THE WIT & WISDOM OF
FOOTBALL

Published in 2012 by Prion
an imprint of the Carlton Publishing Group
20 Mortimer Street
London W1T 3JW

Text compilation copyright © 2012 Nick Holt and Guy Lloyd
Design and layout © 2012 Carlton Books Ltd

ISBN: 978-1-85375-863-8

Printed in China

THE WIT & WISDOM OF
FOOTBALL

**More than 800 amusing, enlightening
and red card-worthy quotations**

PRION

Contents

Superstars

Arsène Wenger has put me down a few times. The annoying thing is, he does it intelligently and I hate that. Sometimes I want to punch him on the nose. *Tony Adams* •1

But how I would love to have been Ali. You can't be better than the best, greater than the greatest, and who wouldn't want to be called that and deserve it. Certainly not a conceited, self-opinionated beggar like me.
Brian Clough admits that there is someone bigger than him •2

I had shortish hair when I came here but I couldn't speak any English and so I couldn't go to the hairdresser to tell him what I wanted done. *Juan Pablo Angel explains his long, lustrous locks* •3

I think Spurs ought to buy a good stock of cotton wool for such poseurs. He can't expect not to be tackled just because Argentina won the World Cup.
Tommy Smith fails to recognise the pedigree of Osvaldo Ardiles •4

Batty would probably get himself booked playing Handel's Largo.
David Lacey in **The Guardian** •5

A real player can always make a monkey out of a gorilla.
Rangers legend Jim Baxter •6

He has transcended the classic footballing context.
He is an integral part of show business. But unlike
Anna Kournikova, he does the business on the pitch.
Marcel Desailly on David Beckham •7

He can't kick with his left foot. He doesn't score
many goals. He can't head a ball. And he can't
tackle. Apart from that he's all right.
George Best •8

Beckham is more of a pop star
than a footballer. *Pele is not impressed by Beckham* •9

Alex Ferguson is the best manager I've ever had at this level. Well, he's the only manager I've ever had at this level.
Beckham whilst at Manchester United •10

Well, I can play in the centre, on the right and occasionally on the left side. *On being asked whether he was a volatile player* •11

I don't think I'm really in a situation to complain, because I consider myself to be privileged to be doing what I do.
David Beckham keeps his feet on the ground •12

Becks hasn't changed since I've known him. He's always been a flash Cockney git.

Ryan Giggs •13

He's absolutely the most gorgeous, gorgeous, gorgeous person. I mean, he's sheer and utter heaven.
Actress Stephanie Beacham after meeting David Beckham on Parkinson •14

If I say Beckham is a "pretty boy", suddenly they say I'm gay, or that Beckham's gay. It's not like that. Nobody's gay! *Diego Maradona plays it straight* •15

Maybe I should just go out and kick one of them for old times' sake.
David Beckham before the 2002 World Cup match against Argentina. He buried the ghost of 1998 in a much more satisfactory way, scoring the only goal of the game from the penalty spot •16

She made all the blokes think she cared as much about football as they did. Who knows? Maybe, just for that one evening, she did.

David Beckham on Victoria's performance at a dinner to celebrate signing for Real Madrid •17

Being thick isn't an affliction if you're a footballer because your brains need to be in your feet.
And Beckham treats a football like he does a wife
— lovingly, with caresses. *Brian Clough* •18

People think I had a square Afro, because it was so big it never fitted into photo frames and the papers and magazines had to crop it that way.

George Berry, 1970s Wolves and Wales star •19

I'm better than Pele.
I can kick with both feet.
George Best •20

When I'm on the field nothing
gives me more pleasure than
making a fool of somebody. *George Best* •21

I'm not a caterer, I'm not really a businessman.
I'm a footballer. Everyone should try and do the
thing he does well; the thing I do well is football.
George Best •22

I don't really class myself as a footballer.
I call myself an entertainer. *George Best* •23

I had nothing but contempt for the so-called hard men. For hard men I always read, men who couldn't play.

George Best •24

The Dutch detailed Neeskens to mark George in that match. Neeskens was some player, but George made a monkey out of him and nut-megged the Dutch star so often that he finished by offering Neeskens a tie-up from his socks to tie his legs together.

Pat Jennings muses on George Best during a Northern Ireland game against Holland •25

So that's what you look like, I've played you three times and all I've seen is your arse.

Welsh left-back Graham Williams to George Best after a 1963 international v Northern Ireland •26

I was getting embarrassing. I didn't want to score any more, so I spent the last twenty minutes at left-back.

George Best gets bashful after scoring six in an FA Cup tie at Northampton •27

The closest I got to him was when we shook hands at the end of the game.

Northampton player Roy Fairfax, who had been marking Best in that game •28

It wouldn't be possible for me to live like a monk to suit the demands of the game. I'd go mad. And now I burn the candle at both ends and drink too much, but I love the game and work hard at it.
George Best in 1970 •29

People always say I shouldn't be burning my candle at both ends, maybe because they don't have a big enough candle.
George Best getting on people's wick •30

They tell me to do so many things… shave off my beard, cut my hair, as if that would make me into what they wanted me to be. Jesus Christ had a beard and long hair and they didn't want to change him. *George Best on being a style icon* •31

13

It's always the same. When they're taking off their clothes they say they hope I don't think they're doing it just because I'm George Best.

Oh, leave it out, George •32

Was I the fifth Beatle? Not really.

George Best •33

Our talking point this morning is George Best, his liver transplant and the booze culture in football. Don't forget, the best caller wins a crate of John Smith's. *Alan Brazil,* Talksport •34

I don't know how it could have happened. I can't imagine him jumping for a ball. I think one of his eyelashes must have come out... I wouldn't know if he was match fit, I've never seen him fit.
George Graham on a head wound sustained by Palace's Thomas Brolin •35

I haven't had the chance to kick a Celtic player for many years.
Ex-Rangers captain Terry Butcher relishes turning out in a veterans' Old Firm game •36

I like to be the tiger roaming the jungle or an eagle soaring over the skies. *Sol Campbell on himself. You what?!!!* •37

The world in which we live is boring. If you're different, you're considered crazy. *Eric Cantona* •38

He's not a tackler. I've told him don't bother tackling because you can't tackle. I'm fed up saying that to him. When he does go into tackles he doesn't know how to do it and ends up getting a booking. *Alex Ferguson spots a flaw in Cantona's game* •39

Eric likes to do what he likes, when he likes, because he likes it — and then fuck off. We'd all want a bit of that.
Howard Wilkinson on the perils of dealing with Cantona •40

I might have said
that, but on the whole
I talk a lot of rubbish.
*A frank Eric Cantona denies
rumours he might return to
football as a coach* •41

Peaks of happiness and depths of pain — just like the chain of mountains in the Alps where I am going to rest and paint.
Eric Cantona on the football season •42

I will never find any difference between Pele's pass to Carlos Alberto in the final of the 1970 World Cup and the poetry of the young Rimbaud. *Cantona on football as art* •43

In football you have an adversary; in cinema that adversary is yourself.
Cantona on his two worlds •44

[While] I know it is irrational I have always been sensitive about my four sons' lack of hair… I have never been able to shake off the feeling that somehow the failure was mine; that I was responsible.
Cissie Charlton takes the rap for Bobby's combover •45

I can't help wondering what I'm going to do when all this ends. *Bobby Charlton in 1970* •46

I don't have lucky signs except my teeth. Sometimes I play with them in and sometimes out. *Martin Chivers* •47

I would like to be a woman, though I don't know why.
Auxerre striker Djibril Cissé gets in touch with his feminine side •48

If you come any closer to me, we might as well get into the same pair of shorts and save a few bob on laundry.
Brian Clough, the player, to Doncaster's Charlie Williams •49

For the players he left behind at Manchester United, there will be one lasting memory of Gary Birtles. His weird, way-out gear… the fancy bow ties, winged collars and spectacular suits that no-one else would wear without the courage of four bottles of wine.
Steve Coppell •50

I wanted to be a garbage collector. He would drive pass my house with his horse and cart. I loved that.
Hernàn Crespo reveals modest childhood ambitions •51

Cruyff sometimes talks nonsense but it is always interesting nonsense.
Johan's biographer Nico Scheepmaker •52

I want the West Ham fans to know that before I finish my career here we'll win something. Otherwise, I'll kill myself. *Paolo di Canio. (They didn't. Paolo moved to Charlton, still in rude health.)* •53

I scored for Liverpool on the opening day of the season… a 'big balls' goal.
Paolo di Canio on big…er…balls •54

If Luis Enrique was a girl, I'd marry him.
Former Spanish national coach Javier Clemente declares his affection •55

You can call me anything, but don't call me late for dinner. *William 'Fatty' Foulke, 24-stone goalkeeper for England, Chelsea, Sheffield United and Bradford* •56

He wears a No. 10 jersey.
I thought it was his position but it turns out to be his IQ.
George Best on Paul Gascoigne •57

We would like him to be our spiritual leader. *Zong Bohong, Gansu team coach, on new signing Paul Gascoigne* •58

One day people might say I was another Ryan Giggs.

George Best turns the tables •59

God gave you intelligence, skill, agility and the best passing ability in the game. What God didn't give you was six studs to wrap around someone else's knee.

Brian Clough to Leeds' Johnny Giles •60

People have got this preconceived idea of me as a fat bastard who can't move.

The generously-proportioned Andy Goram bites back •61

When he plays on snow, he doesn't leave any footprints.

Don Revie on Eddie Gray •62

Take Ruud Gullit. I never liked his arrogance. In fact, I never liked him, but while he was delivering the goods there was no problem. When he lost the plot, he had to go.

Ken Bates, former Chelsea chairman •63

If Glenn Hoddle were any other nationality, he would have had 70 or 80 caps for England.
John Barnes •64

Was it a goal? Did the ball cross the line? Those two questions have haunted me most of my adult life. *Geoff Hurst on 1966* •65

You scored the goal that wasn't a goal.
Franz Beckenbauer to Geoff Hurst, sixteen years after 1966 •66

People look at me and Keane and look back to our Manchester United days and think we are snarling, horrible people. But we are not like that. We are nice guys, family men.
Paul Ince, family man •67

I know all about the Eric Cantonas of this world, with all their dosh. Great players but we're not all born like that. We've not all been so lucky. Some of us have had to work bloody hard to make it this far. *Vinnie Jones* •68

It was one you could stop without arms and legs.

The self-loathing of Bayern keeper Oliver Kahn, after handing Real Madrid a soft goal in the Champions League •69

I'll not go to the fucking World Cup. Now you can have your excuse. It's all Roy's fault. See ye later, lads. *Niall Quinn recounts Roy Keane's parting shot before storming out of the 2002 World Cup finals* •70

My wife said she'd push me if I end up in a wheelchair. *Roy Keane* •71

To call Keegan a superstar is stretching a point. Skill-wise, there a lot of better players around. He's not fit to lace my boots as a player.

George Best gets catty about Kevin Keegan •72

He's been very very lucky — an average player who came into the game when it was short of personalities.

Another typically sniffy assessment of Keegan's worth by Best •73

I've just seen Gary Lineker shake hands with Jürgen Klinsmann – it's a wonder Klinsmann hasn't fallen over.

Ron Atkinson on everyone's favourite diver •74

Denis once kicked me at Wembley in front of the Queen in an international. I mean, no man is entitled to do that, really. *Bobby Robson gets miffed about Denis Law* •75

I don't feel any different to when I was 25, maybe because I've always been this unfit. *Graeme Le Saux* •76

Must devote less time to sport if he wants to be a success. *Quote from Gary Lineker's school report* •77

Jari Litmanen should be made compulsory. *Ron Atkinson* •78

Why am I the best in the world? Because I am, that's all. *Chelsea's man of modesty, Claude Makélélé.* •79

Pele had nearly everything. Maradona has everything. He works harder, does more and is more skillful. Trouble is that he'll be remembered for another reason. He bends the rules to suit himself.

Sir Alf Ramsey •80

My main doubt is whether he has the sufficient greatness as a person to justify being honoured by a worldwide audience. *Pele is peeved after Maradona beats him into second place in FIFA's player of the century poll* •81

What's the point of being the best player in the world if I am not happy? *Maradona's question to God in* **Maradona: The Musical,** *which opened in Buenos Aires in January 2004* •82

People have faith in me, they believe in me as perhaps they believe in God, and I'm not going to contradict them.

Diego Maradona, 2008 •83

I've told him there is always room for bald, grumpy old men in my team.

Gordon Strachan on Saints midfielder Chris Marsden •84

Nah, Pele's the black Rodney Marsh.

Marsh responds to being referred to as 'the white Pele' •85

If I hadn't been a footballer, I'd have been something else; for example, a priest. I mean, something different, something no-one else does. *Rodney Marsh* •86

Somebody would give him the ball and I'd make a run to collect it in the box and it would never arrive. I'd turn around and he'd be juggling it like a bloody seal.

Manchester City's Neil Young on Rodney Marsh •87

It's just like playing alongside Barbara Streisand.

Mike Summerbee on the showmanship of Rodney Marsh, 1973 •88

He was the first great superstar. With only newspapers and radio and TV just starting, everybody knew Stanley Matthews. *Jimmy Armfield* •89

If there were 22 Matthews on the pitch, I'd be out of a job.
Referee Arthur Ellis on the unblemished disciplinary record of Stanley Matthews •90

Playing Stan is like playing a ghost.
Manchester United's Johnny Carey on Stanley Matthews •91

Fitness is confidence.
Stanley Matthews reveals the mystery ingredient •92

I don't know if I was all that good. I never saw myself play, so how do I know?
Stanley Matthews. Well he could look at the trail of top quality fiull-backs in his wake... •93

The maestro appears to be dribbling towards Millet's but could easily swerve across the street to Woolworth's.
Graham Hart, editor of the Guinness Football Encyclopedia, *on the statue dedicated to Stanley Matthews in Stoke* •94

I was thrilled until I heard Ivan Lendl had finished above me.
Ally McCoist, after discovering he was named fifth best-looking sportsman in 1990 •95

Coming to Manchester City, if anything, is more exciting than being at Real Madrid. *Steve McManaman stretches credibility to breaking point* •96

He's a flatterer. And his final ball is pathetic. Pathetic. He fools the public but he doesn't fool me.
Bobby Robson, August 1999, is dismissive of Liverpool and England winger Steve McManaman •97

He is like a PlayStation player. He is the best in the world by some distance.
Arsène Wenger on Messi •98

There should be a law against him. He knows what's happening 20 minutes before anyone else. *Jock Stein on Bobby Moore* •99

It would have been an insult to myself.
Bobby Moore, on suggestions that he should have kicked Pele during their classic World Cup encounter •100

He was the heartbeat of the team in 1966. He was my right-hand man, my lieutenant on the field, a cool, calculating footballer I could trust with my life. *Sir Alf Ramsey pays tribute to Bobby Moore following Moore's death from cancer in 1993* •101

I went to look at him playing for Wealdstone on a stinking night at Yeovil. After eight minutes he put in a thundering tackle and the Yeovil winger landed in my wife's lap. I said to her: 'That's it. I've seen enough. We're going home.'
Bobby Gould recalls the moment he decided to sign Stuart Pearce for Coventry •102

Ask me who is the best right-back in Brazil and I'll say Pele. Ask me about the best left back or the best midfield man, or the best winger, or the best centre-forward... if he wants to be the best goalkeeper, he will be. There is only one Pele.

Former Brazil coach José Saldanha •103

People want to try to find a new Pele. They couldn't do that. You don't find another Beethoven, you have only one Michelangelo. In music you have only one Frank Sinatra and in football you have only one Pele.

Pele, ever the coy one •104

I have come to accept that the life of a front-runner is a hard one, that he will suffer more injuries that most men and that many of those injuries will not be accidental. *Pele* •105

He was laughable, waddling around at a pace barely discernible from a stroll in a manner that suggested some fat geezer who'd won a 'Play a Match with the Hornets' raffle. *Fan Ian Grant describes the four-game career of Mick Quinn* •106

My son Mathieu called it a 'Ninja goal'. This is a result of me playing on his Playstation — it inspires me to try the craziest things. *Laurent Robert on the inspiration behind his overhead kick special against Fulham* •107

He didn't look anything like a professional athlete when I first clapped eyes on him. In fact, there were times when he barely resembled a member of the human race. *Clough on former Forest winger John Robertson* •108

Good strikers can only score goals when they have had good sex on the night before a match. *Romário reveals his pre-match training* •109

I am ugly, but what I do have is charm.

Self-portrait from Ronaldinho •110

I'm not really Jesus Christ. I'm lower down the line.

Ronaldo •111

Wayne mustn't allow himself to become crazy at his own success. He must just enjoy everything about his life and his football. *Advice for Wayne Rooney from Ronaldo* •112

We play at Wembley stadium, not the London Palladium.

England selector's reason for not picking the 'clown prince' Len Shackleton •113

He [Shearer] wouldn't have scored 30-odd a season in the '70s. He'd have had players like me and Tommy Smith kicking great big f ucking lumps out of him and he wouldn't have got a look in. *Ron Harris talking crap* •114

All of us would say 'great player, decent manager', but as man we wouldn't have anything to add. Walking down the corridor in the morning, he wouldn't even say hello. *The departing Keith Gillespie on Blackburn boss Graeme Souness* •115

His left foot is so good he could open a jar of pickles with it.
John Gregory on the extraordinary powers of Steve Staunton •116

There are only two Christs. One plays for Barcelona and the other is in heaven.

Hristo Stoichkov's homage to… himself •117

When Gordon came to Leeds, I was only eighteen and he opened my eyes. He was supposed to be past it but I was amazed at how he lived his life. He even ate seaweed.

Gary Speed on Gordon Strachan •118

There's nobody fitter at his age, except perhaps Raquel Welch.

Praise for Gordon's fitness from Ron Atkinson •119

I wasn't me making those saves, it was God.

Brazil's Taffarel owns up •120

When people ask me what was my biggest thrill
in football, I can't help but think of Raquel Welch
and the day she walked down the touchline at
Stamford Bridge in a pair of skin-tight blue leather
trousers. Much nicer than 'Chopper' Harris.
Frank Worthington fails to keep his eye on the ball •121

I don't like John Terry and I never
have. He's got funny eyes and he's
a cry baby. He's also a Cockney.
Noel Gallagher disses a Manchester City transfer target •122

Isn't he the one who can trap a ball as far as I can kick it?

George Best nicks a line from Big Ron when describing Geoff Thomas •123

When I presented my passport at Immigration they looked
me up and down and said "No, no way." I asked what was
wrong and they pointed at me, laughing "You? A footballer?"
To them it meant big guys in helmets and shoulder pads.
I had to explain I was a soccer player before they let me in.
*The vertically-challenged Mickey Thomas explains one of the pitfalls of
playing in the NAFL* •124

He's not actually a very good player but he's got a lovely smile that brightens up Monday mornings. *Brian Clough considers re-signing Neil Webb* •125

It's funny looking back, but I used to meet Vinnie Jones down the cafe; have sausage, egg, bacon, beans and a fried slice and then go off training. Now it's all pasta, rice and lots of vegetables. *Dennis Wise on a balanced diet* •126

He's fast, strong, sharp and skilful but otherwise he's useless.

Norwich boss Ken Brown on Tony Woodcock •127

Most Dangerous Opponent: My ex-wife.
Frank Worthington answers a questionnaire •128

Not only did we introduce button-down collar shirts into the West Riding which, until then, were unheard of, we also started the Woolly Bully dance craze too. *Frank Worthington, bringing the Swinging Sixties to Yorkshire* •129

I was the first man in Britain to own a tank top. *Frank Worthington on the pressures of being a style guru* •130

I had eleven clubs, twelve if you count Stringfellows.
Frank Worthington on his less than homely lifestyle •131

Down to one man, Don Revie. He preferred the workhorse type of player. *Frank Worthington reflects on his lack of England appearances* •132

One of the only other high points of the season was hoodwinking our beloved neighbours into taking the woeful Abel Xavier off our hands AND paying us half a million pounds for the privilege!

Mark Staniford from Everton fanzine **Speke from the Harbour** •133

The Dark Side

It was partly the head of Maradona and partly the hand of God.

Diego's slant on that infamous goal •134

Cheating and diving is no sin if you win.

Paolo Montero of Juventus fails the audition for Corinthian Casuals. •135

German players have turned the dive into an art form.

FIFA president Sepp Blatter •136

I handled it, I admit it, but I'm not the referee… I played it and we scored, but it was the referee's decision. That's why the Irish all ran to him, not to me.

Thierry Henry produces both mea culpa and feeble excuse in the same sentence. Cue sanctimony by the truckload from the British and Irish Press •137

After this case, I don't think any club will allow a player to miss a drugs test again — and if a bus runs over me tomorrow and that's all we ever achieve then it was worth it for that.

FA chief executive Mark Palios tempts fate after Rio Ferdinand is banned for eight months •138

They have hung him out to dry.

PFA's Gordon Taylor on the Ferdinand drugs-test controversy •139

It is our opinion that the organisation we represent has not only let down one of our team-mates, but the whole of the England squad and its manager. We feel that they have failed us very badly.

Statement from the England squad after agreeing not to boycott a Euro 2004 qualifier in Turkey following Rio Ferdinand's removal •140

Piss in a bottle, you couldn't piss in a bottle.

Spurs fans to Rio Ferdinand after the United defender's eight-month ban for missing a drug test •141

The Football Association are looking for drugs in football. This sort of football is like a drug. It's like pot. You just want more and more of it.

Bob Paisley reveals a surprising comparison •142

This game drives you either to drink or the madhouse… and I'm not going to the madhouse for anybody. *Tommy Docherty •143*

You may have heard this before, but I will respect this liver. After all, it's not mine.

George Best after a transplant. We had, and he didn't •144

I feel awful for the person who died to save George.

Alex Best, wife of George, responds to rumours that he was drinking again after a liver transplant •145

I was fascinated and felt rather sorry for George Best when he went through all his traumas. Fame came to him when he was so young. I've seen it happen to so many young people in the film business.

Elizabeth Taylor sympathises •146

I don't know anybody in a responsible position, or your average working man, who doesn't have a drink, but I was drinking far in excess of what I should have been doing. I had become dependent. *Brian Clough comes clean in his autobiography* •147

What's so great about reality? My reality stank. I was ready for a bender.
Tony Adams •148

I can't remember the last two Championships because I was drinking, so I'll savour every moment of this.
Tony Adams on winning the Premiership with Arsenal in 1998 •149

As far as I am concerned, with each day that I do not take a drink, I will always be a winner. *Tony Adams* •150

It's about the drunken parties that go on for days — the orgies, the birds and the fabulous money.

Peter Storey, ex-Arsenal and England jailbird •151

The spirit he has shown has been second to none.

Terry Venables, commenting on Terry Fenwick's charge for drink-driving •152

Players have got a bigger responsibility than they realise. They have got to discipline themselves… they should only drink, gamble and womanise in moderation. *Barry Fry* •153

Young players today unfortunately often prefer to act like stars in bars rather than on the playing field.

Former French national manager Stevan Kovacs •154

With the foreign players it's more difficult. Most of them don't even bother with the golf, they don't want to go racing. They don't even drink. *Harry Redknapp* •155

I'm finding it difficult to find a girlfriend in Barnsley or to settle into a decent way of life. The girls are far uglier than the ones back in Belgrade or Skopje and drink too much beer.
Georgi Hristov fails to make new friends •156

Without those cigarettes at half-time we could never have gone on. There would have been a mutiny. *French international Georges Bayrou explains the need for relief during a 17-1 hammering from Denmark, 1908* •157

I think I'm the only teetotaller in the Premier League. Team-mates look at me as if I'm an extra-terrestrial.
Rolando Bianchi of Manchester City; perhaps he should've drunk more, might have got injured less •158

Very few of us have any idea of what life is like living in a goldfish bowl. Except of course, for those of us who are goldfish.

Graham Taylor •159

I like to go with him because he doesn't criticise. When I am home, whether we win or lose, he and I go the forest and I feel sometimes as if he will put his paw on my shoulder and say 'Don't worry, Helmut. Next time will be better.'

Former West Germany manager Helmut Schön on deriving motivation from his poodle •160

For a footballer, it's like living in a box. Someone takes you out of the box to train and play and makes all your decisions. I have seen players, famous internationals, in an airport lounge all get up and follow one bloke to the lav. Six of them, maybe, all standing there not wanting a piss, but following the bloke who does, like sheep. *Geoff Hurst* •161

They do everything for you. We're treated like babies, really. So much so that there are some players, not necessarily at this club, who wouldn't know how to check in at an airport. *Lee Dixon* •162

It's like living in a cage.
Rosemary, wife of Pele, in 1970 •163

I sent two players on to a fourth-storey roof to do some slating. We tried to get players down a pit but they wouldn't go because there was this small cavern they had to crawl through. When I was in Scotland I took my YTS people to a building site one day and slapped them in for an eight-hour shift. It made them appreciate they were in an easy life.
Paul Sturrock keeps them on the straight and narrow •164

When I heard about the death threat on Brooklyn I had sympathy for David. I hate him because he plays for Manchester United but that threat was below the belt.
Oasis frontman Liam Gallagher sympathises with the price of fame •165

My life would have ended then if I had gone through with the plan that leapt into my mind: to drive my car at maximum speed and crash.
Nobby Stiles on depression following his playing career •166

More and more footballers' wives will cheat on their husbands because they are never at home. *Emmanuel Petit gets a suspicious mind* •167

I would say that more than 25% of football is gay. It's got to be higher than average. It's a very physical, closed world, a man's world, and you form deep bonds with people you hardly know. *The late Justin Fashanu* •168

I've been called a stupid Paddy over the years. You've just got to ignore it.

David O'Leary •169

I am a Celtic man through and through and so I dislike Rangers because they are a force in Scottish football and therefore a threat to the club I love. *Maurice Johnston in 1988, one year before he joined Rangers* •170

I don't think of foreigners as being professionals in the same sense as us. They're not prepared to give everything in the same way as our fellows. *Bobby Charlton in 1973, a long way from becoming an international ambassador* •171

What I don't understand is how a
Frenchman can be playing for Manchester
United. He's not even from England.

Lord Denning QC overlooks E.C. employment law •172

When an African team takes place in a tournament like this,
the players are always asked two questions by foreign journalists:
"Do you have a witch doctor?" and "Do you eat monkeys?"

Cameroon's François Omam Biyick at the 1990 World Cup finals •173

I knew it wasn't going to be our day when
I arrived at Links Park and found that we had
a woman running the line. She should be at
home making the tea or the dinner for her man
who comes in after he has been to the football.

Albion boss and enlightened modernist thinker Peter Hetherston
on lineswoman Morag Pirie after his side lost to Montrose •174

Off you go, Cantona. It's an early bath for you.

Palace fan Matthew Simmons' own unlikely version of his verbal assault on Eric Cantona, which led to the Frenchman's infamous 'kung-fu' assault •175

We've heard a lot about Cantona's responsibilities. What about analysing the responsibilities of Simmons and every foul-mouthed yob who thinks his £10 admission gives him the right to say what he likes to a man?

Jimmy Greaves raises a rare voice in support of Eric Cantona after the 1995 kung-fu incident •176

All of a sudden the place exploded and this rock came from the other side of the coach. It somehow missed four of the team playing dominoes, grazed Irving Nattrass on the arm, brushed past Frank's face and hit me on the forehead. Then it took a piece out of the card table where Malcolm MacDonald was sitting. My blood was all over the place. It ruined my suit, tie and trousers.

Newcastle striker John Tudor remembers a missile being thrown through the window of the team bus, 1974 •177

They [the fans] were waiting for us at the airport. I had police living in my home for 30 days. One or two of the other players were beaten up and had their cars smashed.

Mexico captain Leonardo Cuéllar recalls the price of failure after the 1978 World Cup •178

The image of the British gentleman along the Belgian coast has given way to one of truculent and drunken youths, throwing cobblestones and wielding sticks.
Belgian lawyer Jean-Marie Berkvens, after Manchester United 'fans' passed through Ostend •179

Their support can be an embarrassment at times, but I'd rather have them as an embarrassment than not at all. *Then Manchester United manager Tommy Docherty on the club's notorious '70s following* •180

I think capital punishment is a great deterrent.
Tommy Docherty offers a solution to the hooligan problem •181

Sun shining. Cheap beer. Got tickets. See you in Istanbul. Diehard England fans.
Postcard to the FA from fans in Macedonia, poking fun at the attempted ticket ban from their own national association •182

If you're so brave, go and enlist to fight in Iraq. Now get out of here.
Terry Butcher confronts England's lunatic fringe at the Stadium of Light •183

I've never been to a club yet that hasn't had a few good fights, it's good for team spirit.
Stuart Ripley on a man's game at Blackburn Rovers •184

I don't really mind that I'm only remembered as a bloke who went in hard. It's better than not being remembered at all. *Ron 'Chopper' Harris* •185

The game you are about to see is the most stupid, appaling, disgusting and disgraceful exhibition of football, possibly in the history of the game.
David Coleman introduces highlights of the 'Battle of Santiago', Chile v Italy, in 1962 •186

Bookings for getting stuck in are OK. Even the odd red card is all right, as long as it is for giving your all. I want my team to be horrible. I want opponents to hate playing us. *Dennis Wise sets out his stall as Millwall player-manager* •187

Basically, I'm a nasty little guy because I always want to win. If I have to boot someone, I'll boot them, simple as that.
Dennis Wise •188

Dennis Wise has made a living out of being a cheat… Dennis tries to be your mate all the time but he quickly forgets that's he's just kicked you in the head, two-footed you or stuck his finger in your ear.
Jason McAteer removes Dennis Wise from his Christmas card list •189

I have this book with two players' names in it. If I get the chance to do them, I will. I'll make them suffer before I pack it in. If I can kick them four yards over the touchline, I will.

Jack Charlton on his notorious 'little black book' •190

Come near me son and I'll break your back.

Ex-Liverpool defender Tommy Smith's self-confessed warning to opposing forwards •191

We've just lost to the hatchet men of Panathinaikos in the first leg of our UEFA Cup-tie. To say it was rough would be like saying that Everest is a pretty big hill.

Ian Rush recalls Juventus v Panathinaikos ruefully •192

In-match dactyl sodomisation.

Spanish FA's official take on the antics of Sevilla's Pablo Alfaro, who was caught on camera inserting his finger into an opponent's rectum •193

Be careful. You're going to die tonight.

Macedonia captain Artim Sakiri to David Beckham before a Euro 2004 qualifier •194

The last time this ground was seen on worldwide television, 'criminals' were being hung from the goalposts and shot in the centre circle.

Gary Mabbutt, member of the footballing taskforce in post-Taliban Afghanistan •195

If you missed a penalty you had your hair hacked off and were spat on by Uday's bodyguards. For every poor pass, you got a punch, and some players were forced to kick concrete balls in a prison yard.

Habib Jaafer, Iraqi midfielder, recalls the horrors of 'coaching' from Saddam Hussein's son •196

The worst they can do is kill me.

Controversial Turkish TV pundit Ahmet Cakar, shortly before being shot five times •197

Eight men will never play again,
who met destruction there,
The flowers of English football,
the flowers of Manchester.

Poem written to those who died at the Munich air disaster •198

What time's the kick-off against Wolves?
I can't afford to miss that one.

Manchester United's Duncan Edwards, on a hospital bed after the
Munich air crash. He died without leaving the hospital •199

You should be dead.

Professor David Lloyd Griffiths, a surgeon, to Manchester City's Bert Trautmann after he had played on in the 1956 Cup Final, ignorant of his broken neck •200

The specialist did these tests, pulled the leg every way imaginable and then took some x-rays. After lengthy analysis he told me, "Your knee is fucked".

Julian Dicks gets blinded with science •201

I've been very lucky about injuries, actually. I've never had any trouble with my legs, or my knees...

Gordon Banks in 1970. Two years later his career finished after he lost an eye in a car crash •202

I was there the night Jock Stein died, and I want to go when I'm in bed with my beautiful young wife.

Graeme Souness on stress •203

I have been a fighter all my life but this one has beaten me. *Former Blackburn manager, Ray Harford, shortly before succumbing to lung cancer* •204

That August was the first time in my football life…
That I hadn't kicked off the season. … My wife took
me paintballing that day, and I shot everybody.
I even shot my own team. My friend's wife ran up
behind me and I turned around and shot her.
She said, "But I'm in your team." And I shot her again.

*David Jones, in a 2002 interview with Brian Viner, explains about dealing
with the disgraceful false allegations about his behaviour in 1999* •205

At the end of the match, Bilic came
to apologise. He knew he'd deprived
me of the Final. And I thought
"Maybe I should hit him now".

*Laurent Blanc on Slaven Bilic, whose shameless playacting in
the 1998 World Cup semi-final caused Blanc's dismissal* •206

...stepping off the edge of the world into silence.

Chris Waddle on taking the penalty that cost England a place in the 1990 World Cup Final •207

View From The Box

John Motson: "Bramall Lane is a fantastic place, and I believe one of the only grounds to host an FA Cup final and Test match cricket."
Mark Lawrenson: "Stay in last night did you, John?"
Sheffield United v Middlesbrough •208

Jaap Stam is like Steve Bould on roller-skates… he's as strong as a tree-trunk, but more mobile.
David Pleat can't see the wood for the trees •209

You're a disgrace to the family.

June Mullery, wife of Alan, in 1968. Mullery had become the first England player to be sent off •210

Sky are overkilling it because they're even boring me, and I'm a fanatic.
Brian Clough •211

At first he told us to wear boxing gloves in bed on Friday nights, then later he would tell us to send the wife to her mother.
Ian St John remembers Bill Shankly's tips for avoiding pre-match relations •212

The day I start worrying about what the press think of me will be the day I pack it in. *Tommy Docherty* •213

Suzuki's got a good engine.
Mark Lawrenson on Japanese striker Suzuki Takayuki •214

They didn't change positions, they just moved the players around.
Terry Venables reveals why his coaching ability is so highly regarded •215

Zoff's alright on the high stuff but on low shots he's been going down in installments.
Ian St. John is critical of Italy's World Cup winning captain •216

They call him Big Ron because he is a big spender in the transfer market. I just call him Fat Ron. *Malcolm Allison, 1993* •217

Wanchope… His full name, Paolo Cesar Wanchope Watson. Why didn't he decide to be called Watson? *Barry Davies* •218

In a restaurant one evening I saw middle-aged citizens rise suddenly and smash glasses and plates and hurl beefsteaks at each other in sheer frenzied delight when they heard over the radio that Uruguay had scored a point. *US author John Gunther gets a culture shock* •219

Back then unless you took a machete out on the pitch you wouldn't get booked.

Jimmy Greaves reflects on a less beautiful game •220

Whelan was in the position he was, exactly.
More incisive stuff from Jimmy Armfield. Where would we be without him? •221

If football were meant to be Art, God wouldn't have invented Carlton Palmer.

Dominik Diamond offers a moment of wisdom •222

He's a little twat, that Totti. I can't see what all the fuss is about. Are there any sandwiches? I'm starving.
Big Ron offers piercing insight during the 2002 World Cup, unaware that the cameras are still rolling •223

The game is about glory. It's about doing things in style, with a flourish, about going out and beating the other lot, not waiting for them to die of boredom.

Danny Blanchflower votes for style over sterility •224

Football's football. If that weren't the case it wouldn't be the game it is. *Garth Crooks* •225

In the words of the old song, 'it's a long time from May to December' but, you know, it's an equally long time from December to May. *Jimmy Hill* •226

I think Arsène Wenger should have been fined several times over for his team's behaviour — forty sendings-off in his first five years as manager is nothing short of a disgrace.
Brian Clough •227

Beckham will take the free kick and he's a world class bender.
German commentary during the 2002 World Cup finals •228

A round ball and a square goal suggest the shape of the Yin and the Yang.
Li Yu (50-130 AD), Chinese writer, describes a prototype of the beautiful game •229

Keegan couldn't have made a bigger impact had he descended into the Kippax hospitality suite on a cloud flanked by horn-blowing Raphaelesque angels and wearing a crown. His arrival at Maine Road was triumphant, only nymphs throwing rose petals into his path were missing.
Bert Trautman's Helmet, *Manchester City fanzine, on Keegan's managerial entrance •230*

This Gaultier-saronged, Posh Spiced, Cooled Britannia, look-at-me, what-a-lad, loadsamoney, sex-and-shopping, fame-schooled, daytime-TV, over-coiffed twerp, did not, of course, mean any harm.

The Daily Telegraph *has a hissy fit about Beckham's sending-off at France '98* •231

If a week is a long time in politics, then for Ron Atkinson's Manchester United, the last seven days have been an equinox. *Stuart Hall* •232

That's not the type of header you want to see your defender make, with his hand. *Ron Atkinson* •233

I've lost count of how many corners there have been. Lincoln have one and Crystal Palace seventeen.
Ron Jones, Radio 5 Live •234

I will die a Catholic,
I will die an Arsenal fan
and I will die a Tory.
Former Conservative MP Chris Patten •235

Brazil, the favourites — if they are the favourites, which they are…
Brian Clough gets tongue-tied •236

It's those bums on the sports pages I hate most.*Brian Clough on the press* •237

Achtung! Surrender

Mindless Mirror *headline before the England v Germany semi-final in Euro '96* •238

Two soccer points to no score.

A US website reports the nation's 2-0 victory over Mexico at the 2002 World Cup •239

I never miss *Match of the Day*.

Cardinal Basil Hume, 1978 •240

If United fail to beat Wolves tonight, will the last person out of Elland Road please turn off the lights?

Back page of the Yorkshire Post *before Leeds' vital relegation clash (they won 4-1)* •241

Chris Waddle is off the pitch at the moment, exactly the position he is at his most menacing.

Gerald Sinstadt •242

John Bond has bought a young left-sided midfield player who, I guess, will play on the left side of midfield. *Jimmy Armfield* •243

You can see the ball go past them, or the man, but you'll never see both man and ball go past at the same time. So if the ball goes past, the man won't, or if the man goes past they'll take the ball.

Ron Atkinson on Zen and the Art of Dribbling •244

73

Like all the great dictators, from de Gaulle to Thatcher, he stayed on a little too long.

Gazzetta dello Sport, *Italy's leading sports paper, on Brian Clough* •245

If Jennings had been available on that memorable occasion when the Roman met the Etruscans, Horatius surely would have had to be satisfied with a seat on the substitutes bench.

The Guardian *gets carried away after Pat Jennings has a decent game at Leeds* •246

'…famous for missing open goals and for the inexorable precision with which he would find the goalpost'.

Italian newspaper's verdict on Luther Blissett's lone season for Milan •247

You know when I say that things happen in matches. Well, it just happened there.

Ron Atkinson •248

Every British male, at some time or other, goes to his last football match. It may well be his first football match.

Martin Amis fails to appreciate the beautiful game •249

One of the best socialists I've ever met.
Former Labour Party leader Michael Foot on Brian Clough •250

He's what is known in some schools as a fucking lazy thick nigger.
Ron Atkinson's thoughtless and offensive parting shot aimed at Chelsea's Marcel Desailly •251

Swan Lake on turf.

Kenneth Wolstenholme's description of the 1960 European Cup Final at Hampden Park; Real Madrid 7-3 Eintracht Frankfurt •252

To say that these men paid their shillings to watch twenty-two hirelings kick a ball is merely to say that a violin is wood and catgut, that Hamlet is so much paper and ink. For a shilling the Bruddersford United AFC offered you conflict and art…'
JB Priestley in **The Good Companions,** *1929* •253

England have been beaten by the Mickey Mouse and Donald Duck team.

US press comment after the Americans humbled England 1-0 at the 1950 World Cup •254

Wembley is just one huge satsuma at the moment.

John Inverdale talks fruity nonsense as the Dutch fans brighten Wembley •255

The new West stand casts a giant shadow over the pitch, even on a sunny day.

Chris Jones in the **Evening Standard** •256

The Brazilians aren't as good as they used to be, or as they are now.

Kenny Dalglish •257

Our football comes from the heart, theirs from the mind.

Pele, when asked the difference between football in South America and Europe •258

That's bread and butter straight down the goalkeeper's throat. *Andy Gray* •259

You are filth and you smell of manure...

Belgian coach Robert Waseige loses it with his country's press at the 2002 World Cup •260

Long Live the Mother who Gave Birth to You

Headline in Spanish sports' daily Marca *after Spain's 4-3 defeat of Yugoslavia at Euro 2000* •261

It's only twelve inches high. It is solid gold. And it undeniably means England are the champions of the world. *Kenneth Wolstenholme* •262

John Harkes going to Sheffield, Wednesday.

Headline from the New York Post, *1993. Don't get it? They just don't teach grammar these days...* •263

United are hated, are they? I haven't noticed that. I must be out of touch. *Denis Law catches up with the rest of the country* •264

Soon there were bodies everywhere, blue with death… I had come to photograph Platini and had ended up photographing war.

Photographer Eamonn McCabe reveals the horror of the Heysel disaster •265

He carried on alone, blew out his cheeks, and beat Tilkowski with a terrible left footer.

Brian Glanville describes Geoff Hurst's goal in the 1966 World Cup Final •266

I'm going to sue Alan Hansen as he used to make me head all the balls. If I get Alzheimer's in ten years, I'm going to take civil action against him.

Mark Lawrenson on former centre-back partner Alan Hansen •267

Who's the fat bloke in the number eight shirt?

Headline in The Guardian, *following the discovery of football boots worn by Henry VIII •268*

We've been playing for an hour and it's just occurred to me that we're drawing 0-0 with a mountain top.
Scottish radio commentator Ian Archer despairs of his team's performance against San Marino •269

He's probably already forgotten about that bang on the neck.
BBC commentator Kenneth Wolstenholme, on Manchester City goalkeeper Bert Trautmann after the 1956 Cup Final. Trautmann's neck was later found to be broken •270

Malcolm Macdonald uses the same conditioner as me.
Bob Ferris (Rodney Bewes) boasts to an unimpressed Terry Collier (James Bolam) in '70s sitcom Whatever Happened to the Likely Lads? •271

This fellow Tardelli, he's likely to leap out of the TV at us. He's put more scar tissue on people than the surgeons at Harefield hospital. *Jimmy Greaves gets scared* •272

I received the ten shillings in expenses, returned to my cosy middle-class house and turned my back on pro-football to embark on a proper job. *Stuart Hall on the moment he swapped the playing field for the microphone* •273

Wife-beating is a despicable activity. But I do not see how Glenn Hoddle could have excluded Paul Gascoigne from the England team on this. Hoddle is a manager not a judge of morals.

Johnny Giles in the **Daily Express** *sweeps Gazza's behaviour under the carpet* •274

If every manager in Britain were given his choice of any one player to add to his team some, no doubt, would toy with the idea of Best; but the realists, to a man, would have Bremner.

John Arlott in **The Guardian** *on Billy Bremner* •275

Football, wherein is nothing but beastly fury and extreme violence, whereof proceedeth hurt, and consequently rancour and malice do remain with them that be wounded.

Thomas Elyot, **Book of the Governor,** *1531 (Vinnie Jones wasn't even born for another 434 years)* •276

It's just a round thing you kick to another player, hmmm? Isn't it? Wasn't it? Er...

Tactical genius Ron Manager reveals his philosophy •277

Hagi has got a left foot like Brian Lara's bat.
Don Howe •278

When you look up into the crowd, what do you think about?
Question at a press conference during a tour of China by Manchester United •279

The game should be a two-act play with
22 players on stage and the referee as director.
Referee Ken Aston gets theatrical •280

I was sorry to see O'Leary leave. So sad — in the appropriately
mournful words of the late Ian Curtis, "How can something
so good not function no more". He brought back life into the
club, then threw it all away by publishing his memoirs.
Mark Monk of Leeds fanzine **Toellandback** *sums up the O'Leary era* •281

He might be a great action man, but when it comes to football he hasn't got a bloody clue.
Kevin Beattie on Sylvester Stallone, during shooting of footie film **Escape to Victory** •282

The difference between right and wrong is often not more than five metres.
Johan Cruyff •283

We love Brazil because they are Braziiiiiiiiiiil.

Alex Bellos puts the samba into that second syllable •284

Argentinian police are hunting for Diego Maradona's missing penis.

The plastic device – used by the player to cheat drugs tests in the 90s – disappeared while on loan from a Buenos Aires museum. The Star *report the ultimate piss-take* •285

At half-time the game's virginity was still intact.

Clement Freud •286

A woman on her wedding day – nervous, out of position and hoping everything would soon be over so she could go up to the bedroom.

Spanish newspaper Marca *gives its verdict on Fabien Barthez' performance for Manchester United against Real Madrid* •287

Football is a game you play with the ball, not the legs.

David Ginola explains his work-rate •288

It's real end-to-end stuff, but unfortunately it's all up at Forest's end. *Chris Kamara* •289

Who'd want a girl who plays football but can't make chapattis? *Jes is upbraided by her family during Brit-flick* **Bend it Like Beckham** •290

Which planet are you from? I am going to cry! Oh, my God! How beautiful soccer is! What a goal! Diego Maradona! You make it seem so easy! I am crying, forgive me please!
Argentine commentator Victor Hugo Morales celebrates the second against England at the 1986 World Cup. •291

Back then, you were made if your photo and an interview appeared in *Shoot*. Now all some players want is to get into *Hello* magazine.
Niall Quinn on youngsters today •292

We've sold our birthright down the fjord to a nation of seven million skiers and hammer throwers who spend half their lives in darkness…

Charmless rant from the Daily Mail's *Jeff Powell, after Sven-Göran Eriksson's appointment as England coach* •293

Both sides have scored a couple of goals and both sides have conceded a couple of goals. *Peter Withe. So it's 2-2 is it, Peter?* •294

The Anfield shrine with its long queue wrapped round the ground provokes comparison with Lenin's tomb; there is the same reverence, the same sense of a religious need fulfilled.

John Sweeney describes Anfield after Hillsborough •295

A penalty is a cowardly way to score.

Pele, 1966•296

Bob Wilson [needs] to go on a crash course in basic communication techniques so he'll grasp that if you ask someone a question you have to give them longer than five seconds to answer before interrupting.

One of the list of demands printed by fanzine When Saturday Comes *in its 1996 tenth birthday issue* •297

In my lifetime, there have been three British footballers who would walk into St. Peter's All Time XI. They are Tom Finney, George Best and John Charles.

Michael Parkinson •298

I watch programmes on current affairs and I see maybe a twenty-minute piece on Bangladesh or the German elections. That's very interesting but you go into the pub and people aren't talking about the elections in Germany or the poverty in Bangladesh.
Brian Moore on the importance of football to the nation •299

Our programme's biggest contribution has been to humanise the stars. These blokes are normal, not toys that appear at three every Saturday afternoon to be put away two hours later.

Brian Moore on the show he hosted for many years, ITV's **The Big Match** •300

The game of football is like that. You win and you lose.
Pope Paul VI grasps the rudiments during an audience with Lazio in 1968 •301

Nothing would stop me going to the Cup Final unless I was dead. And if I was dead, I'd want my ashes taken there.

MP and Chelsea fan Tony Banks before his team's Final appearance in 1997 •302

He hit the post, and after the game people are going to say, well, he hit the post. *Jimmy Greaves* •303

I'm not going to pick out anyone in particular but Jay Jay Okocha should not be the captain of a football club. *Rodney Marsh* •304

That was an inch-perfect pass to no one.
Ray Wilkins •305

Put shit hanging from a stick in the middle of this passionate crazy stadium and some will tell you it's a work of art. It's not: it's shit hanging from a stick.
Jorge Valdano isn't impressed by the Champions League semi final between Liverpool and Chelsea •306

Hello my sharks, welcome to the funeral.

An under-pressure Claudio Ranieri at a press conference before a crucial Champions League match against Monaco •307

Bergkamp's just been on another plane.

Peter Drury, obviously not describing Dennis's travel arrangements •308

They're just as bad as benefit scroungers. It's just a higher class of sponger.
Cheryl Cole (who has no need to scrounge off of anyone) on Footballers' Wives •309

Lord Nelson! Lord Beaverbrook! Sir Winston Churchill! Sir Anthony Eden! Clement Attlee! Henry Cooper! Lady Diana! Maggie Thatcher can you hear me? Maggie Thatcher! Your boys took a hell of a beating! Your boys took a hell of a beating! *Bjørge Lillelien, Norwegian commentator, after his countrymen overcome England in a 1981 World Cup qualifier* •310

We've lost hundreds of soldiers (in Iraq), 100,000 people have been killed and nobody in this country gives a toss. Yet John Terry sleeps with some bird and everyone's up in arms.
Jimmy Greaves •311

My wife is in Portugal with the dog, so the city of London is safe, the big threat is away.

José Mourinho mocks the authorities attempts to impound his Yorkshire terrier •312

Gary Lineker: "So Gordon, if you were English, what formation would you play?"
Gordon Strachan: "If I was English I'd top myself!"
A classic exchange from the 2006 World Cup studio •313

You've been shite, son, in your daft pink boots.

Richard Keys isn't impressed with Theo Walcott, and forgets the microphone is still on in 2010; he would make a similar, more costly error later that year •314

The first half was end-to-end stuff. In contrast, in this second half it's been one end to the other. *Lou Macari* •315

Own Goal

We didn't underestimate them. They were a lot better than we thought.

Bobby Robson after England squeezed past Cameroon in a World Cup Quarter final •316

The man is United — cut him and he bleeds red.

Alan Brazil on Alex Ferguson •317

Football, it's an old, funny game.

Gianluca Vialli nearly gets his order in the right words •318

Brazil – they're so good it's like they are running around the pitch playing with themselves.

John Motson •319

The underdogs will start favourites for this match.

Craig Brown •320

Ireland is not a bar of chocolates.

Georgian international Alexander Rekhviashvili sets his sights on the Premier League rather than the Emerald Isle •321

One year I played fifteen months.
Franz Beckenbauer turns the clock forward •322

The whole thing was unreal, like a freak of nature.
Alf Ramsey on surrendering a two-goal lead to Germany,
which spelled England's exit from the 1970 World Cup •323

Steven Carr has hit a small blimp.
Glenn Hoddle •324

I have seen Manchester United so many times on
the television this season and they were playing
really poor football, really rubbish. There is no
doubt we are the best football team in England.
Patrick Viera after United have beaten Arsenal to the title, May 2003 •325

You get bunches of players like
you do bananas, though that
is a bad comparison. *Kevin Keegan* •326

91

I don't really like the North. It's always raining, it's very cold and I don't like all those little houses.

Frédéric Kanouté ensures a warm reception on away grounds north of Watford •327

I am so sorry. I have been unable to sleep after what happened... I promise I will replace this unhappy situation with happy things.

José Antonio Reyes, after his first goal for Arsenal is past his own keeper •328

...when Flitcroft played for the A team, he had 'footballer' written all over his forehead.

Colin Bell •329

I spent four indifferent years at Everton, but they were good years. *Martin Hodge* •330

For those of you watching in black and white, Spurs are in the yellow strip. *John Motson* •331

I'm not convinced that Scotland will play a typically English game.

Gareth Southgate •332

If there wasn't such a thing as football, we'd all be frustrated footballers.

Mike Lyons •333

All the Leeds team are 100% behind the manager, but I can't speak for the rest of the squad.

Brian Greenhoff •334

England now have three fresh men with three fresh legs. *Jimmy Hill* •335

I was inbred into the game by my father.

David Pleat keeps it in the family •336

I'd give my right arm to get back into the England team. *Peter Shilton cuts off his nose...* •337

It wasn't a bad performance but you can't tell whether it was good or bad. *Jimmy Hill* •338

Terry Venables has literally had his legs cut off from underneath him three times while he's been manager. **Barry Venison** •339

Hierro has been magnificent for the Spaniards tonight.
TV pundit Dion Dublin gives his verdict. One problem; Hierro wasn't playing •340

We are now in the middle of the centre of the first half.
David Pleat •341

It's the end-of-season curtain raiser. *Peter Withe* •342

I'll never play at Wembley again,
unless I play at Wembley again.
Kevin Keegan •343

If you just came into the room
and didn't know who was who,
you'd obviously say Newcastle
looked the most likely to score.
Terry Paine •344

It's a football stadium in the truest sense of the word.
John Motson •345

We had ten times as many shots on target as Bolton,
and they had none at all… *Bobby Robson fails the maths* •346

If history is going to repeat itself I think we
can expect the same thing again. *Terry Venables* •347

95

Jesus was a normal, run-of-the-mill sort of guy who had a genuine gift, just as Eileen [Drewery] has.
Glenn goes away with the fairies •348

They've missed so many chances they must be wringing their heads in shame. *Ron Greenwood* •349

Merseyside derbies usually last 90 minutes and I'm sure this one won't be any different. *Trevor Brooking* •350

Forlan gets the ball inside the box, on the edge of the box and put it away from inside the box.
George forgets he's on air and not in the pub •351

Shaun Wright-Phillips has got a big heart. It's as big as him, which isn't very big, but it's bigger.
Kevin Keegan •352

It may have been going wide, but nevertheless it was a great shot on target. *Terry Venables* •353

Zola's got two feet.
David Pleat wins Big Ron's spotter's badge... •354

He held his head in his hands as it flashed past the post. *Alan Brazil* •355

The goals made such a difference to the way this game went. *John Motson* •356

Venison and Butcher are as brave as two peas in a pod. *John Sillett* •357

He was as game as a pebble.
David Webb's commentating career sinks like a stone •358

Once Tony Daley opens his legs, you've got a problem. *Howard Wilkinson* •359

Most of the players will be wearing rubbers tonight.
Gary Lineker •360

They've come out with all cylinders flying.
Luther Blissett •361

Apart from their goals, Norway wouldn't have scored.
Terry Venables •362

It was a definite penalty but Wright made a right swansong of it. *Jack Charlton* •363

I'd be surprised if all 22 players are on the field at the end of the game – one's already been sent off. *George Best* •364

The World Cup is a truly international event. *John Motson* •365

The World Cup is every four years, so it's going to be a perennial problem. *Gary Lineker* •366

If England are going to win this match, they're going to have to score a goal. *Jimmy Hill* •367

Seaman, just like a falling oak, manages to change direction.
John Motson •368

Well, I've seen some tackles Jonathan, but that was the ultimatum. *Alan Mullery* •369

For such a small man Maradona gets great elevation on his balls. *David Pleat* •370

We were a little bit outnumbered there, it was two against two. *Frank McLintock* •371

I don't think there's anyone bigger or smaller than Maradona. *Kevin Keegan* •372

It's end to end stuff,
but from side to side.
Trevor Brooking •373

Women should be in the kitchen, the discotheque
and the boutique but not in football.
Ron Atkinson forgets to engage brain before opening mouth •374

Hearts are now playing with a five-man back four.
Alan McInally •375

All the cul-de-sacs are closed for Scotland.
Joe Jordan •376

The Scots have really got their
hands cut out tonight. *Trevor Francis* •377

The club has literally exploded.
Ian Wright •378

He's like all great players but
he's not a great player yet.
Trevor Francis •379

The ball goes down the keeper's throat where it hits him on the knees to say the least. *Ron Atkinson* •380

That would have been the icing on his start.
David Pleat •381

Barnsley have started off the way they mean to begin. *Chris Kamara* •382

The game is balanced in Arsenal's favour.
John Motson •383

We didn't have the run of the mill.
Glenn Hoddle •384

If there's one thing Gus Uhlenbeek's got,
it's pace and determination. *Ray Houghton* •385

It's his first cap, so he's not got a lot of experience at this level.
Brian Marwood •386

…and for those of you watching without
television sets, live commentary is on Radio 2.
David Coleman •387

If they play together, you've got two of them.
Dion Dublin •388

The 3-5-3 system isn't working for them.
Eamonn Dunphy goes up to eleven •389

He didn't get booked for the yellow card.
Frank Stapleton •390

He hasn't been the normal Paul Scholes today, and he's not the only one. *Alvin Martin* •391

Scotland don't have to score tonight, but they do have to win.
Billy McNeill •392

He can't speak Turkey, but you can tell he's delighted.
Kevin Keegan •393

…the Derby fans walking home absolutely silent in their cars. *Alan Brazil* •394

He hits it into the corner of the net as straight as a nut.
David Pleat •395

He'll take some pleasure from that, Brian Carey. He and Steve Bull have been having it off all night.
Ron Atkinson •396

In some ways, cramp is worse than having a broken leg.

Kevin Keegan •397

It seems that they're playing with one leg tied together.

Kenny Sansom •398

The substitute is about to come on. He's a player who was left out of the starting line-up today.

Kevin Keegan •399

My dad always told me to keep my mouth shut. Now I've realised I've reached the stage where I must learn to do it in big tournaments. I know I'll never be sent off playing for England.

David Beckham, shortly before France '98 •400

I don't think anyone enjoyed it. Apart from the people who watched it. *Alan Hansen* •401

This is a real cat and carrot situation.
David Pleat •402

We haven't had a strategic free kick all night.
No one's knocked over attackers ad lib.
Ron Atkinson •403

It's like the Sea of Galilee,
the two defenders just parted.
Mark Lawrenson •404

Even if he had scored for Alaves, it would have made no difference to the scoreline. *Gerry Armstrong* •405

Michael Owen isn't the tallest of lads, but his height more than makes up for that.
Mark Lawrenson •406

When it comes to the David Beckhams of this world, this guy's up there with Roberto Carlos. *Duncan McKenzie* •407

> Some of the goals were good, some of the goals were sceptical. *Bobby Robson* •408

Borussia Moenchengladbach 5 Borussia Dortmund 1.
So, Moenchengladbach win the Borussia derby.
Gary Newbon •409

> These managers all know their onions and cut their cloth accordingly. *Mark Lawrenson* •410

The midfield picks itself; Beckham, Scholes, Gerrard and A.N. Other. *Phil Neal* •411

The Belgians will play like their fellow Scandinavians, Denmark and Sweden.
Andy Townsend •412

And Arsenal now have plenty of time to dictate the last few seconds.
Dave Bassett •413

Chelsea last won away on April Fool's Day. Now it's Boxing Day, another great religious holiday.
Dominic Johnson •414

And what a time to score! 22 minutes gone.
John Motson •415

To be fair, I don't think Les Ferdinand was fouled there. I think he went over on his own ability. *Alan Mullery* •416

Romania are more Portuguese than German.
Barry Venison •417

I think you and the referee were in a minority of one, Billy. *Jimmy Armfield* •418

Let's close our eyes and see what happens.
Jimmy Greaves •419

108

It was a fair decision, the penalty, even though it's debatable whether it was inside or outside the box.
Bobby Charlton •420

Paul Gascoigne has recently become a father and been booked for over celebrating. *John Motson* •421

Batistuta gets most of his goals with the ball.
Ian St John •422

It is a cup final and the one who wins it goes through. *Jimmy Hill* •423

People will look at Bowyer and Woodgate and say 'Well, there's no mud without flames.'
PFA chairman Gordon Taylor •424

They can crumble as easily as ice cream in this heat.
Sammy Nelson •425

We sometimes think of Arsène Wenger as a general media population. *Rodney Marsh* •426

The lad got over-excited when he saw the whites of the goalposts' eyes. *Steve Coppell* •427

The time in the world has gotten shorter so it doesn't take so long to get to Australia. *Phil Neal bids to be the new Dr. Who* •428

There are so many teams now down at the bottom of the Third Division. The FA really has to do something about it. *Peter Lorimer* •429

This game could go either way. Or it could be a draw. *Peter Lorimer stays on the fence* •430

I was here at Maine Road when City lost 4-0 to Wimbledon, but they could have been 2-0 up after five minutes, and if they had been, the final score might just have been different. *Jim Beglin* •431

If they hadn't scored, we would have won.
Howard Wilkinson •432

It's a tense time for managers. They have to exhume confidence. *Gary Lineker* •433

We got the winner with three minutes left but then they equalised. *Ian McNail* •434

He looks as if he's been playing for England all his international career.
Trevor Brooking •435

I've never even heard of Senegal.
From Paul Gascoigne's mercifully brief spell as an ITV panelist during the 2002 World Cup finals •436

Michael Owen is not a diver. He knows when to dive, and when not to. *Steve Hodge* •437

Roy Keane didn't go through the book with a fine toothbrush. *Tony Cascarino* •438

The first two-syllable word I learned when I was growing up was 'discretion'. *Eamonn Dunphy* •439

It's so vital if you can win the game one-nil rather than lose it one-nil. *Billy Bonds* •440

The fans like to see Balde wear his shirt on his sleeve. *Kenny Dalglish •441*

You're not sure if the ball is going to bounce up or down.
Frank Stapleton •442

There is still nothing on the proverbial scoreboard.
John Motson •443

PSV have got a lot of pace up front. They're capable of exposing themselves. *Barry Venison •444*

They've got one man to thank for that goal, Alan Shearer. And they've also got to thank referee Chris Wilkie.
Chris Kamara •445

Solskjaer never misses the target. That time he hit the post.
Peter Schmeichel •446

Djimi Traore had to adapt to the English game and he did that by going out on loan to Lens last season. *Ian Rush •447*

The Swedish back four is amongst the tallest in the World Cup. Their average height is 7 foot 4. *Chris Waddle* •448

He talks not probably enough yet, due to the experience he hasn't got. *Chris Waddle* •449

He was in a no-win situation, unless he won the match. *Murdo MacLeod* •450

Eighty per cent of teams who score first in matches go on to win them. But they may draw some. Or occasionally. *David Pleat* •451

A game is not won until it's lost. *David Pleat* •452

He's hardly been on the pitch as many times as he's played. *Alvin Martin* •453

Peter Beardsley has got a few tricks up his book. *Ian Snodin* •454

The fact that Burnley got beat here already will stick in their claw. *Mark Lawrenson* •455

Nearly all the Brazilian supporters are wearing yellow shirts. It's a fabulous kaleidoscope of colour.
John Motson •456

Every time they attacked, we were memorised by them.
Charlie Nicholas •457

He signals to the bench with his groin.
Mark Bright •458

It's slightly alarming the way Manchester United decapitated against Stuttgart. *Mark Lawrenson* •459

Bruce has got the taste of Wembley in his nostrils.
John Motson •460

Manchester United have hit the ground running, albeit with a three-nil defeat. *Bob Wilson* •461

They get to about 30 yards out and then everything goes square and a bit pedantic. *Charlie Nicholas* •462

Bridge has done nothing wrong, but his movement's not great and his distribution's been poor. *Alan Mullery* •463

He's not the sharpest sandwich in the picnic.
Tony Cascarino •464

He's such an honest person it's untrue.
Brian Little •465

Had we not got that second goal the score might well have been different. *David Pleat* •466

I like to think it's a case of crossing the 'i's and dotting the 't's. *Dave Bassett* •467

The important thing is, he shook hands with us over the phone.
Alan Ball •468

Tempo. Now, there's a big word.
Barry Venison •469

He's had two cruciates and a broken ankle. It's not easy that. Every player attached to the club is praying the boy gets a break. *Alex Ferguson on Wes Brown* •470

Winning all the time is not necessarily good for the team.
John Toshack •471

That's an old Ipswich move – O'Callaghan crossing for Mariner to drive over the bar.
John Motson •472

All strikers go through what they call a glut, where they don't score goals. *Mark Lawrenson nutmegs himself* •473

We had a pedantic tempo in the first half. We tittered on the edge of nervous stability.
Sam Allardyce laughs off a Bolton performance, sort of •474

No-one hands you cups on a plate.
Terry McDermott •475

If you can get through the first round, you have a good chance of getting into the next one. *Nigel Worthington* •476

Not quite the first half you might have expected,
even though the score might suggest that it was.
John Motson •477

Tor's got a groin strain and he's playing with it.

Alex McLeish predicts premature short-sightedness for Tor André Flo •478

With eight or ten minutes to go, they were able to bring Nicky Butt back and give him fifteen to twenty minutes. *Niall Quinn* •479

He lacks that confidence which he possesses.
Martin O'Neill •480

A bit of retaliation there, though not actually on the same player.
Frank Stapleton •481

I'd like to have seen Tony Morley left on as a down-and-out winger. *Jimmy Armfield* •482

We signed to play until the day we died, and we did. *Jimmy Greaves* •483

He's only a foot away from the linesman, or should I say a metre in modern parlance. *Jimmy Armfield* •484

In football, you can never say anything is certain. The benchmark is 38-40 points. That has always been the case. That will never change. *Steve Bruce* •485

Matches don't come any bigger than FA Cup quarter-finals. *Neil Warnock* •486

It was a continuance of what we have seen this season. That is, various clubs beating each other.
Ron Noades •487

And I suppose they [Spurs] are nearer to being out of the FA Cup now than any other time since the first half of this season, when they weren't ever in it anyway. *John Motson* •488

The gelling period has just started to knit.
Ray Wilkins knits jelly •489

It's Arsenal 0 Everton 1, and the longer it stays like that the more you've got to fancy Everton to win. *John Motson* •490

Statistics are there to be broken.
Chris Kamara •491

Leeds have only had one shot on target, which may well have been the goal. *Andy Gray* •492

As long as you have a hole in your arse, you'll never make a footballer.
Fulham manager Malcolm Macdonald to teenage triallist Niall Quinn. To the best of our knowledge Niall never had his arsehole sealed up, and yet… •493

The unexpected is always likely to happen. *John Motson* •494

Whoever wins the Championship today will win the Championship no matter who wins. *Denis Law* •495

Unfortunately, we don't get a second chance. We've already played them twice. *Trevor Brooking* •496

The match has become quite unpredictable, but it still looks as though Arsenal will win the Cup. *John Motson* •497

The beauty of cup football is that Jack always has a chance of beating Goliath. *Terry Butcher* •498

The Arsenal defence is skating close to the wind.
Jack Charlton •499

Whether that was a penalty or not, the referee thought otherwise. *John Motson* •500

We looked all around Europe for people with any credentials, but it is a fact that anyone who is any good was already tied up with a job.
Alan Sugar unveils Christian Gross as manager of Tottenham with a ringing endorsement before later announcing... •501

The referee is wearing the same yellow-coloured top as the Slovakian goalkeeper. I'd have thought the UEFA official would have spotted that, but perhaps he's been deafened by the noise of this crowd.
John Motson •502

The Blackburn crowd have been saturated by fifty thousand Newcastle fans. *Brian Little* •503

I've been asked that question for six months. It's not fair to expect me to make such a fast decision on something that has been put upon me like that. *Terry Venables* •504

I was a young lad when I was growing up.
David O'Leary •505

I watched the game, and I saw an awful lot of it.
Andy Gray •506

I saw him kick the bucket over there, which suggests he's not going to be able to continue.*Trevor Brooking* •507

I know that Gareth Barry has been told by Howard Wilkinson to take a long hard look at these with his left foot. *John Motson* •508

Kevin Keegan said that if he had a blank sheet of paper, five names would be on it. *Alvin Martin* •509

Sol Campbell there, using his strength. And that's his strength — his strength.

Kevin Keegan on top form •510

Not So Daft After All

When you get up at six o'clock in the morning to go to work and it's pitch black outside, and you know it will still be dark when you come home at night, that's when you appreciate being a professional footballer. *Ian Wright counts his blessings* •511

Half at Highbury, half at White Hart Lane.
Ian Wright's answer to the question: "Where would like your ashes scattered?" •512

This is Britain in the 1990s. A Labour-supporting multi-millionaire who liked a beer with the lads and put his wealth into football seems like an authentic hero. *Matthew Engel on the late Chelsea director Matthew Harding* •513

In the course of time it will be said that Maradona was to football what Rimbaud was to poetry and Mozart to music.
Eric Cantona •514

When the seagulls follow the trawler, it is because they think sardines will be thrown into the sea.
Eric Cantona's famous observation on press behaviour •515

Imagine Franz Beckenbauer trying to play for Watford. He'd just be in the way.

Frank McLintock disdains Graham Taylor's long-ball approach, 1982 •516

You'll never meet Des Walker.

Journalists' running gag. Des was not known for talking to the press •517

You could hardly be worse off sitting on your food and eating your seat. The nutritional value could not be any lower, nor the view any worse. *Colman's Football Food Guide delivers its verdict on Wembley* •518

MADR.I.P.

Headline in 1999 from Catalan's Sport, *following Real Madrid's elimination from the Champions League* •519

Thank goodness at least one member of the Hill family knows something about football!

Gary Lineker reviews the footie-based novel, Penalty Chick, *by Jimmy Hill's wife Bryony* •520

Fenerbahce's Saracoglu stadium, a ground with more flares than a Showaddywaddy convention.

The Observer's take on a tendency for the volatile in Turkey •521

It was like asking Frank Sinatra to sing in front of three-dozen people!

Jimmy Greaves on playing to small crowds at the 1962 World Cup finals •522

Footballers have a very short career… a few seasons in the spotlight is followed by retirement, death and then a stint on Sky Soccer Saturday. *Jeff Stelling, host of Sky Soccer Saturday, attempts not to get his contract renewed* •523

The only person, who, when he appears on television, makes daleks hide behind the sofa. *Peter Beardsley described in the* Observer Sport Monthly •524

The only ground that looks the same in black and white as it does in colour.

David Lacey of the **The Guardian** *describes Hampden Park* •525

Until you've seen a match in Tegucigapla your soccer education isn't complete. The atmosphere in the stadium makes the Kop seem like a meeting of the noise-abatement society.
Chris Davies of the **Observer** *describes a World Cup qualifier between Mexico and Honduras* •526

Why didn't you just belt it, son?

Gareth Southgate's mother offers coaching tips after her son's penalty miss at Euro '96 •527

As a land mass, Luxembourg might best be described as 'pert'... home advantage counts for little, when corners have to be taken from well inside Belgium.
When Saturday Comes *writer Andy Lyons explains the Duchy's footballing shortcomings* •528

Sheedy was sent off, apparently for accusing the referee of vaginal duplicity.

The Guardian *notes Kevin Sheedy's sending-off during a Chelsea v Everton cup-tie* •529

I just opened the trophy cabinet. Two Japanese prisoners of war fell out.
Tommy Docherty •530

Apparently he finds the yellow and red a little too gaudy – which is pretty rich coming from someone who used to arrive on stage wearing a pink mohair jockstrap and a pair of angel's wings.

Journalist Giles Smith on Elton John's dislike of a new Watford kit •531

Tuning into Radio 5 Live to listen to the football, there is nothing worse than having to endure reports from rugby matches… I am not the only one who wants to jail football fans who sing *Swing Low Sweet Chariot.*
When Saturday Comes *contributor Ken Sproat speaks for armchair fans everywhere* •532

If, as every Englishman suspects, the Scots ingest a weakness for hyperbole with their mother's milk, Ally MacLeod would seem to have been breast-fed until he was fifteen.

Hugh McIlvanney searches for explanations following Scotland's failed 1978 World Cup campaign •533

That's great. Tell him he's Pele and get him back on.

Partick boss John Lambie, after discovering that dazed striker Colin McGlashan did not know who he was •534

It's a rat race, and the rats are winning.

Tommy Docherty •535

The Beatles are a good example. In the beginning, like them, we had enthusiasm together. But later the pleasure was gone, we didn't want to play together any more. *Former Ajax midfielder Gerrie Mühren on the break-up of the legendary Seventies' team.* **Brilliant Orange** •536

I would buy some bad players, get the sack and then retire to Cornwall. *Sheffield United boss Neil Warnock considers if he was manager of Sheffield Wednesday* •537

Half a million for Remi Moses? You could get the original Moses and the tablets for that price! *Tommy Docherty disapproves of goings-on at his former club* •538

I would like to thank Scotland and Mr McLeod for the team they presented us with. *Peru manager, Marcos Calderon, with a nod to Ally's team selection in the 1978 World Cup Finals* •539

Hartson's got more previous than Jack the Ripper. *Harry Redknapp* •540

Brains? There's a lot of players who think manual labour is the Spanish president. *Tommy Docherty runs through the after-dinner routine* •541

We've watched them twice, and seen a few videos. I didn't see them 38 times though, like McCarthy says he watched us. I don't think that's possible. I did my maths you see. That's 38 times 90 minutes — that's two months and the draw was only three weeks ago.

Belgium boss Georges Leekens tells his Irish counterpart Mick McCarthy to pull the other one •542

I thought it was like Barack Obama getting the Nobel Peace Prize after eight months as US President.

Fabio Capello's response to David Beckham winning Man of the Match
after a half-hour cameo against Belarus •543

There is one, but the best manager in the world is there and he isn't giving up yet.

Martin O'Neill's candid reply to the question at his first press conference
for Celtic, "Is there any othe club you would have left Leicester for?" •544

I came away wondering to myself what we had been doing all these years.

England's Tom Finney after the famous 6-3 drubbing by Hungary at Wembley in 1953 •545

It was like playing people from outer space.

England defender Syd Owen on the same match •546

We reckon he [Carlton Palmer] covers every blade of grass on the pitch, mainly because his first touch is crap.

David Jones •547

My wife said to me in bed, "God, your feet are cold."
I said, "You can call me Brian in bed, dear."

Pillow talk from Brian Clough •548

When I was admitted to the heart unit, somebody sent me a 'get well' telegram that said "we didn't even know you had one".

Brian Clough •549

Women run everything. The only thing I've done within my house in the last twenty years is recognise Angola as an independent state.
Brian Clough admits he finally defers to someone •550

I had a walk along the River Trent today. As you know, it's my normal practice to walk on it.
On being made a freeman of Nottingham, Brian Clough address the civic reception in his honour •551

Oh, I dunno. I've just won a championship last year and just knocked Liverpool out. It's terrible. It's been awful. The chairman should get rid of me. *Harry Redknapp can afford to joke after Portsmouth knock Liverpool out of the FA Cup.* •552

I've had more clubs than Jack Nicklaus.
Tommy Docherty •553

If I walked on water, my accusers would say it is because I can't swim.
Ex-German coach Berti Vogts •554

I've been called a sadist, a sergeant major, a Glasgow tough who lashes his players. I'm not in the game to make friends. I don't want to be Tommy Docherty the popular manager. I want to be Tommy Docherty the success.
But it never quite happened •555

I'm not giving secrets like that to Milan. If I had my way I wouldn't even tell them the time of the kick-off.
Bill Shankly, on being asked before a European Cup semi-final whether he was changing his team •556

My team-mates advised me to visit the city first. I went to have a look at Middlesbrough and decided I was better off in Parma. *Antonio Benarrivo avoids the culture shock* •557

You'll have to stop writing about the bleedin' figures and concentrate on the football now. But, before you do, having picked up five points from the previous fifteen games, that's six points from four undefeated since I arrived. *New Forest boss Joe Kinnear spells out his early form at a press conference* •558

An offence against the dignity of work.
Vatican statement on Milan's payment of £13m to Torino for Gianluigi Lentini •559

Congratulations for buying Ronaldo? Thanks, but my grandma could have discovered a talent like that. *Frank Arnesen on bringing Ronaldo to PSV Eindhoven* •560

I've been given the number 35 shirt to reflect my age. *Steve Claridge muses on his shirt number at Millwall* •561

I prefer players not to be too good or clever at other things. It means they concentrate on football. *Former Spurs' boss Bill Nicholson* •562

We were caviar in the first half, cabbage in the second.
Phil Thompson on a Jeckyll-and-Hyde display by Liverpool at Charlton •563

Football makes me emotional. Not many people can explain what it's like when you play all season and you get to Wembley or somewhere, and at the end you and all the lads walk down the tunnel while the other lot are doing the lap of honour.
Norman Hunter on some nearly days at Leeds •564

I've only been booked twice this season. The last one was for doing an impression of the linesmen…
I got the other yellow card for winking.
Alan Shearer sheds that 'boring' tag •565

Leeds United? Most people imagine us as an evil-looking bunch of characters with black capes and handlebar moustaches. *Johnny Giles on being part of Revie's Leeds* •566

Football is not art, but there is an art to playing good football.

Rudi Krol **Brilliant Orange** •567

There is no medal better than being acclaimed for your style.

Johan Cruyff **Brilliant Orange** •568

I went to the Chelsea training ground and watched Claudio Ranieri, who's a fantastic Italian coach, do exactly the same thing we were doing at Plymouth Argyle. Coaches are coaches. The secret of it all really is man management.
Paul Sturrock •569

A medal from Princess Di and a kiss from Sam Hammam and with no disrespect to either, you wish it could have been the other way round!
Vinnie Jones on receiving his FA Cup winners' medal in 1988 •570

It is like loading a bullet into the chamber of a gun and asking everyone to pull the trigger. Someone will get the bullet, you know that, and it will reduce them to nothing. Fairness is not even an issue. *Christian Karembeu on penalty shoot-outs* •571

All that I know most surely of morality and
the obligations of man I owe to football.
Albert Camus •572

I understand why they would chant Judas at me,
but if we're going to get Biblical, then maybe it should
be Moses, because we led them from the wilderness.
Owen Coyle on the response from Burnley fans after he left for Bolton •573

Pele… has done more for goodwill and friendship between nations than all of the ambassadors put together.

J.B. Pinheiro, Brazilian ambassador to the UN •574

"What do you think of Brazil?" "I think he's a great player."

Kenny Dalglish 'misunderstands' a journalist at the 1982 World Cup finals •575

I have no interest in gardening. If I did I would probably plant my
flowers in a 4-4-2 formation. *Tommy Docherty* •576

When people come to assess my career, I do not want them to judge me on victories or defeats. I want them to say: he played the game, he was fair, he didn't cheat the players or the crowd. If I never cheated them, I never cheated anybody. *Bill Shankly* •577

David Batty is quite prolific, isn't he? He scores one goal a season, regular as clockwork. *Kenny Dalglish* •578

I am not condoning the dirty play that Wimbledon have such a name for: but why are their longball tactics considered immoral and a disgrace to the game? If you get beaten in a running race, it is no good complaining that the other person didn't run gracefully enough.
Simon Barnes defends The Crazy Gang •579

He comes with his usual health warning for centre halves.
Keith Gillespie on Blackburn colleague Mark Hughes •580

I have no complaints about Thierry Henry being named double player of the year. He deserved it and I voted for him myself.
Ruud van Nistelrooy at the end of the 2002/03 season •581

D'you think you'll be a player when your voicc breaks?

Billy Bremner to Alan Ball during Scotland's 1967 victory against the Auld Enemy •582

You'd have a got a better view from the stand.

Bolton's Frank Worthington to Terry Butcher of Ipswich after lifting the ball over his head •583

We, Lakeside United, are a Sunday amateur club and have been formed three years. Despite being of great repute, we need a little more punch and think that Mr Greaves will fit the bill adequately.

Hopeful letter from Lakeside United in Thurrock to Milan, offering to return Jimmy Greaves to the nation, 1961 •584

If you were a racehorse, they'd shoot you.

Francis Lee implies that the 37-year-old Mike Summerbee is past his best •585

How does it feel to be a navvy among artists?

Millwall's Eamonn Dunphy to Villa's Trevor Hockey •586

Short back and sides, please.

Ray Parlour in his compulsory session with Eileen Drewery, 1998 •587

142

You'd better win this one lads. I need the bonus.
I've got a wife, two kids and a budgie to keep.

Alan Gilzean motivates the Tottenham team •588

Some teams take failure and use it as a reason to come back stronger.
That is what Germany appear to have done. Other teams use failure
as an excuse for more failure and it becomes a mental block.
Franz Beckenbauer. D'you think he means England in the second instant? •589

When you have friends in the game you want them to do well… but not as well as you.

*Colin Harvey, upon getting the manager's job at Everton, on his predecessor and former
team-mate Howard Kendall. Kendall was to succeed Harvey three years later* •590

The most interesting guy I ever met was the ex-soccer player Jimmy Johnstone,
from Celtic. What a character; the voices, the rhythms, the speech patterns …
And he'd sing to me like Neil Diamond. He'd drink and come on to women.
I named a dog after him. *American actor Robert Duvall on a Celtic legend* •591

He's so tiny, I half expected him to come
out with a school satchel on his back. If he
had, I'd have trodden on his packed lunch.

Wimbledon's Andy Thorn marvels at the diminutive stature of Juninho •592

We could have something special here. If he can develop some pace, he's going to be some player. *Terry Owen on his young son Michael* •593

Wayne [Rooney] is only seventeen but Sachin Tendulkar didn't become an Indian cricket legend by him being kept back because of his age. *Gary Neville* •594

The simplest solution is to stop the ball getting to Ronaldo in the first place. If the ball does get to him, we have to make sure he has no space to turn or knock the ball into. And if that doesn't work, we'll have to tie his shoelaces together.
John Collins on Scotland's game plan before the1998 World Cup opener •595

I don't give a damn about records. Kylie Minogue makes records.
Sunderland's Jason McAteer shrugs off the club's losing streak •596

I'd rather buy a *Bob the Builder* CD for my two-year-old son.
McAteer reviews Roy Keane's autobiography •597

Yes, I swear a lot. But the advantage is that having played abroad, I can choose a different language to the referee's.
Jürgen Klinsmann •598

I just want to ask you fellas; is (sic) there any diving schools in London? *Jürgen Klinsmann to the English press on arriving at Spurs* •599

Next, a man who's fulfilled every schoolboy's dream. He's won the Double, captained England and driven his car into a wall at very high speed. Ladies and gentlemen, Tony Adams! *Tony is introduced to the audience on the Kumars at No. 42* •600

I've been looking for new kitchen curtains for a long time. *Norwegian keeper Erik Thorstvedt after swapping goalkeeping jerseys with the flamboyant Jorge Campos of Mexico* •601

When you have played at Millwall and seen some of the things that go on there, this should be nothing I can't handle. *Kasey Keller takes the USA v Iran World Cup clash in his stride* •602

Do you want me to buy a left-back or help save children's lives? I'm not going to do both… go and look in that hospice and have a look at the kids — that's where my money is going.

Robbie Williams reacts to suggestions that he might slip a few bob to home-town Port Vale •603

If the crowd only wants to come and watch models then they should go and buy a copy of *Playboy*.

Norwegian international Lise Klaveness with a sideswipe at Sepp Blatter •604

It's a top club but it's not a top, top, top club.

Jimmy Floyd Hasselbaink on Chelsea's position in footballing society •605

The first thing I will do is negotiate a pay rise, give myself a ten-year contract, and then sack myself. *Graham Turner on the perks of owning and managing Hereford United* •606

It'll never replace plastic.

Ray Harford, whose QPR team played on an artificial surface, is unimpressed with the real thing •607

Jesus, I only wanted you to pass the salt.

Roy Keane reacts to a tactical talk from Tony Adams at a UEFA dinner •608

We used to joke in the United dressing room that he was the only player in the League who had to have turn-ups on his shorts.
George Best on the diminutive Bobby Collins of Leeds •609

Someone asked me last week if I missed the Villa. I said 'No, I live in one.' *David Platt on swapping Birmingham for Bari* •610

In Glasgow half the football fans hate you and the other half think they own you.
Tommy Burns •611

Watch a Brazilian pass the ball. No lofted centre from the wing for him, no forty-yard long-balls that need only to be a yard out to be wasted. *Tom Finney* •612

147

Even when they had Moore, Hurst and Peters, West Ham's average finish was about seventeenth. It just shows how crap the other eight of us were.

Harry Redknapp •613

He was involved in both and spent so much time on the ground I was wondering when his funeral would be held.

FIFA assessor Keith Cooper on Ashley Cole's role in red cards for Leeds' Danny Mills and Lee Bowyer •614

My goodness! You have been out of the Premiership a long time. *Ron Atkinson puts down an Ipswich steward who asked for identification* •615

It is the first time, after a match, that we've had to replace divots in the players.

Big Ron after Manchester United's encounter with a somewhat physical Valencia •616

I just bumped into Cyrille Regis and I said 'What's all this about you finding God? You worked with him at West Brom for four years'.

Ron Atkinson on Cyrille Regis's born-again Christianity •617

He's the worst finisher since Devon Loch. When he's in a clear shooting position he's under orders to do just one thing... pass. *Ron on Carlton Palmer* •618

If that's Junior Baiano, I wouldn't like to meet Senior Baiano.
Ron Atkinson with a commentary box gem •619

Five days thou shalt labour, as the Bible says. The seventh day is the Lord thy God's. The sixth day is for football.
Anthony Burgess •620

Football is all very well as a game for rough girls, but is hardly suitable for delicate boys.
Oscar Wilde •621

Football is the opera of the people.

Stafford Heginbotham, former Bradford City chairman •622

The rules are very simple, basically it is this: if it moves, kick it. If it doesn't move, kick it until it does.
Soccer writer Phil Woosnam puts it in a nutshell •623

In a world haunted by the hydrogen and napalm bomb, the football field is a place where sanity and hope are still unmolested. *Stanley Rous, 1952* •624

People say his first touch isn't good, but he usually scores with his second.

Wolves manager Graham Turner offers an assessment of Steve Bull •625

I'm out at the moment, but should you be the chairman of Barcelona, AC Milan or Real Madrid, I'll get straight back to you. The rest can wait. *Joe Kinnear's answering machine* •626

As we went out on the pitch he handed me a piece of paper. It was the evening menu for the Liverpool Royal Infirmary.

Jimmy Greaves recalls an Anfield encounter with Tommy Smith •627

Rumour has it that when Julian Dicks moved to Liverpool he picked up the number 23 shirt because it said Fowler on it. *Football writer Kevin Baldwin* •628

It's bloody hard work being true to the real values.
Bill Shankly •629

There's no such thing as staleness. It's just a name given to the state of mind of some players. It doesn't exist if their will is fresh.
Tommy Docherty •630

All a manager has to do is to keep eleven players happy. The eleven in the reserves. The first team are happy because they're the first team. *Rodney Marsh* •631

It's bad players who are the luxury, not the skillful ones.
Danny Blanchflower, on hearing whispers that he might be a liability •632

I'd like to get ten goals a season but the authorities don't normally let me play for a whole season.

Vinnie Jones •633

I believe that international football between representative teams is on the way out. Its days are numbered and it will disappear completely just as soon as we get a full programme of international football at club level. *Jimmy Greaves in 1962* •634

Look laddie, if you're in the penalty area and aren't quite sure what to do with the ball, just stick it in the net and we'll discuss your options afterwards. *Bill Shankly* •635

Playing against English clubs is like when your mother forced you to eat vegetables when you didn't like it. You have to suffer a bit if you want to be strong. *Hernán Crespo in his pre-Chelsea days* •636

Our goalscoring is like ketchup, you never know how much is going to come out of the bottle.

Club Brugge manager Trond Sollied •637

I think that clocking into a factory would be the worst thing in the world. All you could say to the man next to you is 'What's in your sandwich, Charlie?'.
Rodney Marsh muses on his escape, 1967 •638

Chris Cattlin is a very complex mixture of a man who could alternate between Mussolini and Bambi depending on which day you caught him.
Frank Worthington's verdict on his ex-Brighton manager •639

I'm a people's man, a player's man. You could call me a humanist.
Bill Shankly •640

153

It's a tremendous honour. I'm going to have a banana to celebrate.
Gordon Strachan on being voted Footballer of the Year in 1991 •641

I don't know how you face people after that. When you go and speak to your mates and they ask what did you contribute to the game and you say "I fell, I fell like a big Jessie".
Gordon Strachan pours scorn on the antics of Bolton's Mário Jardel •642

That'll be the Samaritans. They usually call me this time of day.

Gordon Strachan after a mobile going off at a Southampton post-match press conference •643

We're not doing bad. What do you expect us to be like? We were eighth in the league last year, in the Cup Final and we got into Europe. I don't know where you expect me to get to. Do you expect us to win the Champions League?
Gordon Strachan is peeved after a reporter's careless question •644

I've got more important things to think about. I've got a yoghourt to finish by today. The expiry date is today. That can be my priority rather than Agustin Delgado.
Gordon Strachan has little time for his misfit striker •645

If a Frenchman goes on about seagulls, trawlers and sardines, he's called a philosopher. I'd just be called a short Scottish bum talking crap.
Gordon Strachan •646

Dear Dad,
I hope you don't mind but I don't want to be a Spurs fan any more.
Love Sam

Letter from nine-year-old Sam Curtis to journalist father Adrian, after Spurs surrendered a 3-0 half-time lead to Manchester City in an FA Cup replay •647

Manager-speak

I'll try not to apologise too much for the game but I'm glad I got in for free.

Leicester manager Micky Adams defends a dire nil-nil at Southampton •648

Arsenal claim they can't be bullied. They can. Our record says they have a problem with us.

Sam Allardyce in his time at Bolton on Arsenal's reluctance to mix it •649

There are scientists who will tell you that spirit, because it can't be measured, doesn't exist. Bollocks. It does exist.

Sam Allardyce •650

We will win the European Cup. European football is full of cowards and we'll terrorise them.

Malcolm Allison on the Manchester City side of the early '70s. They didn't •651

We wrote to Manchester United asking for permission to use their name and got a letter back from Sir Matt Busby telling us to go ahead.

Brian Askuez, manager of the other Manchester United in Gibraltar •652

At least we were consistent – useless in
defence, useless in midfield and crap up front.
Ron Atkinson raves after Villa lose 3-0 at Coventry •653

I always make sure I write Atkinson D on
the teamsheet. Sometimes I wonder if I'm
making a mistake. *Ron Atkinson as Villa boss wonders*
whether selecting Dalian is a good idea •654

How can anybody call this work? People in this game
don't realise how lucky they are. You drive to the ground,
play a few five-a-sides, then have lunch.
Ron Atkinson on his managerial lot at Aston Villa •655

We've got absolutely no interest in him. We've got a goalkeeper
with a better trick — he stops the ball with his hands.
Ron Atkinson on transfer links with the flamboyant
Colombian goalkeeper René Higuita •656

The only relaxed boss is Big Ron. He had me
drinking pink champagne — before the match.
Harry Redknapp •657

157

Did you know Alan Ball's missus used to come and watch us in training? One day she said to Keith Curle, 'You should have been tighter at the back.' *Manchester City's Nicky Summerbee on having to endure advice from the manager's wife* •658

There is no place for a gay in my team. And I could easily spot one if he tried to get into my team. Gays are no good and can not be role models for our youth. *Croatian coach Otto Baric fails to come out of the closet* •659

I just felt that the whole night, the conditions and taking everything into consideration and everything being equal, and everything is equal, we should have got something from the game, but we didn't. *John Barnes loses it at Celtic* •660

You weigh up the pros and cons and try to put them into chronological order. *Dave Bassett* •661

And I honestly believe we can go all the way to Wembley, unless somebody knocks us out. *Dave Bassett* •662

At the moment, we couldn't hit a cow's arse with a banjo.

Dave Bassett is not upbeat about Sheffield United •663

We are a very good average team.

Franz Beckenbauer is nearly modest •664

They had a dozen corners, maybe twelve. I'm guessing.

Craig Brown •665

It was a very simple team talk. All I used to say was:
"Whenever possible, give the ball to George Best."

Matt Busby on United's tactics •666

159

There's a rat in the camp trying to throw a spanner in the works.

Brighton boss Chris Cattlin in metaphor madness •667

He told you how to dress. He told you how to do your hair.
Pre-war Arsenal and England international Eddie Hapgood on the influence of legendary manager Herbert Chapman •668

It was a game we should have won. We lost it because we thought we were going to win it. But, then again, I thought there was no way we were going to get a result there.
Jack Charlton •669

If in winning we could only draw we would be fine.
Jack Charlton •670

I've seen them on television on a Sunday morning most days of the week. *Jack Charlton* •671

Jack cracks me up. He makes out he's not really interested in football and tells the whole world he's gone fishing. But we know what he's thinking about when he's fishing. Football. *Johan Cruyff on Jack Charlton* •672

I wouldn't say I was the best manager
in the business, but I was in the top one.
Brian Clough •673

Rome wasn't built in a day but I wasn't on that particular job.
Brian Clough •674

If a player had said to Bill Shankly
"I've got to speak to my agent" Bill would
have hit him. And I would've held him down.
Brian Clough •675

Coaching is for kids. If a player can't trap a ball and
pass it by the time he's in the team, he shouldn't be
there in the first place. I told Roy McFarland to go and
get his bloody hair cut — that's coaching at this level.
Brian Clough •676

In this business, you've got to be a
dictator or you haven't got a chance.
Brian Clough •677

Look at your players prior to the coach leaving and count the hearts. If there are less than five, don't bother setting off. A team's no good without courage. *Harry Storer, a mentor of Brian Clough, offers sound advice* •678

You can throw all those medals in the bin, because you won them all by cheating.
Brian Clough on his arrival at Leeds •679

The only person certain of boarding the coach for the Littlewoods Cup Final is Albert Kershaw, and he'll be driving it.
Brian Clough keeps his team-sheet close to his chest •680

If the BBC ran a Crap Decision of the Month competition on *Match of the Day*, I'd walk it.
Rare humble offerings from Brian Clough on Forest's relegation in 1993 •681

I've seen big men hide in corridors to avoid him. He can make you feel desperate for his approval.
Martin O'Neill on Brian Clough •682

At the end of the day, it's all about what's on the shelf at the end of the year.

Steve Coppell proves that his time at university wasn't wasted •683

I'm not going to make it a target but it's something to aim for.
Steve Coppell •684

Attilio Lombardo is starting to pick up a bit of English on the training ground. The first word he learned was wanker.
Steve Coppell on the rarefied atmosphere at Crystal Palace •685

No complaints. I thought it was a soft penalty award anyway.
Liverpool manager Kenny Dalglish is magnanimous after John Aldridge's penalty miss costs them the 1988 Cup Final •686

Chester made it hard for us by having two players sent off.

John Docherty •687

It's the only stadium in the world I've ever been in that's absolutely buzzing with atmosphere when it's empty and there isn't a soul inside.
Tommy Docherty on Old Trafford •688

When the television people asked me if I'd like to play a football manager in a play, I asked how long it would take. They told me 'about ten days' and I said 'That's about par for the course'. *Tommy Docherty* •689

Football management these days is like nuclear war: no winners, just survivors.
Tommy Docherty •690

We are Lego. Many bricks that fit together to make a smooth wall.
Poland manager Jerzy Engel before their first World Cup match in 2002. They lost •691

I admire the English mentality because you are so strong, so hard working. But we have talent.
Sven-Göran Eriksson on English football in 1991, after his Benfica side eliminated Arsenal from the European Cup •692

My greatest challenge is not what's happening at the moment, my greatest challenge was knocking Liverpool right off their fucking perch. And you can print that. *Alex Ferguson* •693

It's a disgrace, but I don't expect Wenger to ever apologise, he's that type of person.
Alex Ferguson on his perennial adversary after the infamous "tunnel incident" in 2005 •694

If you are that full of yourself, as Arsenal are, it can come back to haunt you.

Alex Ferguson on Arsenal's eight-point lead in the Premiership •695

Arsène is a winner. …It was a competitive situation, not just between Arsène and myself, but on the pitch… It was quite volatile, but they are different teams now.
Alex Ferguson reassesses his relationship with Arsène Wenger in 2009 •696

It's just the two of us. We'll probably ride out in the sunset together.
Sir Alex Ferguson on his relationship with Wenger •697

Mr Ferguson is killing the referees. He is the only manager in the English league that cannot be punsihed for these things.
Rafa Benitez' famous rant about Fergie's antics in January, 2009 •698

They are just a small club with a small mentality. All they can ever talk about is us.

Alex Ferguson on Manchester City in 2009 •699

Don't swap shirts with those dirty bastards.

Alex Ferguson on Feyenoord after a Champions League tie •700

They fiddled the draw so we wouldn't get to the Final on our own ground.

Alex Ferguson cries foul after United were drawn against Real Madrid in the 2003 Champions League quarter-final •701

The lads ran their socks into the ground.

Alex Ferguson •702

If we can play like that every week, we'll get some level of consistency.

Alex Ferguson •703

It's a conflict of parallels.

Alex Ferguson •704

It was particularly pleasing that our goalscorers scored tonight.

Alex Ferguson •705

Coventry, in all honesty, never really looked like scoring.
Alex Ferguson misses the finer points of a 3-2 defeat at Highfield Road •706

Everyone knows that for us to get a penalty we need a certificate from the Pope and a personal letter from the Queen.
Alex Ferguson answers criticism that United get more than their fair share •707

Do you think I would get into a contract with that mob? No chance, exactly. Christ almighty, I wouldn't sell them a virus, let alone Cristiano Ronaldo.
Alex Ferguson shows his disaffection with Real Madrid's transfer methods, before selling them Cristiano Ronaldo a few months later •708

Squeaky-bum time.
Alex Ferguson gives an anal soundbite on the end-of-season run-in •709

I could see Fergie's face turning purple. "Club car?" he yelled. "You've got more chance of getting a club bike."
Ryan Giggs on how not to ask Alex Ferguson for a set of wheels •710

Football… bloody hell.
Fergie after the 1999 Champions League Final, later used as the title of a biography on him by Patrick Barclay •711

167

We've got a monster round our neck
after beating England, but we must feed it.

Socceroos' coach Frank Farina gets an appetite after Australia beat England •712

What I said to them
at half-time would be
unprintable on the radio.

Gerry Francis •713

Give him his head and he'll
take it with both hands or feet.

Bobby Gould •714

That's not the worst reception I've ever
had – did you ever see me as a player?

Bobby Gould reacts to a demonstration against him at the Hawthorns •715

The one thing I didn't expect is the way we didn't play.

George Graham •716

Playing another side could be an
omen, but I don't believe in omens.

George Graham •717

Bryan Robson. Well, he does what he does and his future is in the future.
Ron Greenwood turns astrologer •718

Being given chances and not taking them, that's what life is all about.
Ron Greenwood •719

In comparison, there's no comparison.
Ron Greenwood •720

I think everyone in the stadium went home happy, except all those people in Romania.
England manager Ron Greenwood after a World Cup qualifier in Romania •721

He's gone in there with studs up and has cut someone
in half, but I don't want to criticise him.
John Gregory •722

I've always loved left-footed players. There's something about them that is very sexy.
John Gregory •723

I understand the fans complaining.
They wanted a big name and got me.
An unusually modest John Gregory on his appointment at Aston Villa •724

Compared to the preparation Brazil have had,
we are motorways behind them, absolute motorways.
Still, it's no use crying over spilt milk, we'll just have
to get a new cow. *Glenn loses the plot, and his audience •725*

You can't compare two players who are
different because they're not the same.
Glenn Hoddle •726

He was a player that hasn't had to use his legs,
even when he was nineteen years of age because
his first two yards were in his head. *Glenn Hoddle •727*

I think in international football you have to be able to handle the ball.
Glenn Hoddle •728

To put it in gentleman's terms, if you've been out for a night and you're looking for a young lady and you pull one, you've done what you set out to do. We didn't look our best today but we've pulled. Some weeks the lady is good looking and some weeks they're not. Our performance today would have been not the best looking bird but at least we got her in the taxi. She may not have been the best looking lady we ended up taking home but it was still very pleasant and very nice, so thanks very much and let's have coffee.
Ian Holloway after a QPR win over Chesterfield •729

If the water stands still in the pond, it starts to stink.
QPR boss Ian Holloway goes all Cantona in explaining a desire for new signings •730

I couldn't be more chuffed if I were a badger at the start of the mating season.
Ian Holloway after a Cup victory over Cardiff •731

If you're a burglar, it's no good poncing about outside somebody's house, looking good with your swag bag ready. Just get in there, burgle them and come out. I don't advocate that obviously, it's just an analogy. *Holloway after a heavy defeat at Crystal Palace* •732

I love Blackpool. We're very similar. We both look better in the dark.
Ian Holloway •733

In the first-half we were like the Dog and Duck, in the second-half we were like Real Madrid. We can't go on like that. At full-time I was at them like an irritated Jack Russell. *Ian Holloway* •734

I'd rather do that than build chicken sheds no-one wanted!
Ian Holloway after Blackpool reached the Championship play-offs in 2009; he spent ayear out of the game building hen-houses •735

Reporter: Ian, have you got any injury worries?
Holloway: No, I'm fully fit, thank you. *Ian Holloway* •736

In football you need to have everything in your cake mix to make the cake taste right. One little bit of ingredient that Tony uses in his cake gets talked about all the time is Rory's throw. Call that cinnamon and he's got a cinnamon flavoured cake. It's not fair and it's not right and it's only a small part of what he does.
Ian Holloway claims there is more to Stoke's style than … er… cinnamon •737

It's all very well having a great pianist playing but it's no good if you haven't got anyone to get the piano on the stage in the first place, otherwise the pianist would be standing there with no bloody piano to play.
Holloway on the role of the defensive midfielder •738

I have such bad luck at the moment that if I fell in a barrel of boobs I'd come out sucking my thumb. *Ian Holloway* •739

You never count your chickens before they hatch. I used to keep parakeets and I never counted every egg thinking I would get all eight birds. You just hoped they came out of the nest box looking all right. I'm like a swan at the moment. I look fine on top of the water but under the water my little legs are going mad.
Ian Holloway •740

Every dog has its day — and today is woof day! Today I just want to bark.

Ian Holloway after Blackpool clinched promotion from the third tier •741

It was not a mistake, it was a blunder.
Gérard Houllier •742

You can't say my team aren't winners. They've proved that by finishing fourth, third and second in the last three years. *Gérard Houllier* •743

At the end of the day, the Arsenal fans demand that we put eleven players on the pitch. *Don Howe* •744

Up front we played like world beaters — at the back it was more like panel-beaters.
Paul Jewell after his Wigan side drew 3-3 with Tottenham •745

I don't read everything I read in the press.
Dave Jones •746

It's nice for a bluenose to come here and win. I'm going to have a pint now and a gloat. *Childhood Everton fan Dave Jones celebrates a Southampton victory at Anfield* •747

It was the first four goals that cost us the game.
Southampton manager David Jones picks up a bleedin' obvious award •748

The stupid, bloody rule. Is he offside or not? We don't know what to do with it. You can't coach against it. It's rubbish. *Wolves manager David Jones speaks for us all as the offside law becomes more nonsensical •749*

Why not? Hopefully the boss will be around for a few more years but yeah, it has crossed my mind. *Roy Keane on the manager's job at Old Trafford •750*

I have a number of alternatives and each one gives me something different. *Kevin Keegan •751*

In the dressing room at the interval, I told the lads that we'd be playing for pride and that I'd be praying for a miracle. *Keegan's team-talk to Manchester City, 3-0 down to Spurs with ten men at White Hart Lane. They won 4-3 •752*

175

There's a slight doubt about only one player and that's Tony Adams, who definitely won't be playing tomorrow.

Kevin Keegan •753

You need 88 points for the title and we've got 61 at present with sixteen games to go, but if you set targets you limit yourself. *Kevin Keegan* •754

You can't do better than go away from home and get a draw.

Kevin Keegan •755

I know what is round the corner, I just don't know where the corner is. But the onus is on us to perform and we must control the bandwagon. *Kevin Keegan* •756

The only way we will get into Europe is by ferry.

Kevin Keegan acknowledges the task ahead after his return to Newcastle United •757

But I'll tell you — you can tell him now if you're watching it — we're still fighting for this title, and he's got to go to Middlesbrough and get something, and… And I tell you honestly, I will love it if we beat them — love it.

Kevin Keegan's legendary rant at Alex Ferguson as his side let a 12- point lead in the title race slip •758

I told him Newcastle was nearer to London than Middlesbrough, and he believed me.

Kevin Keegan on persuading the geographically challenged Rob Lee to join Newcastle •759

Age isn't important except on tombstones and birth certificates. He can still do the business.

Tranmere manager John King after signing 35-year-old John Aldridge in 1991 •760

I can count on the fingers of one hand ten games where we've caused our own downfall. *Joe Kinnear* •761

These managers who buy players from videos, I find that impossible to believe. You never see the bit where the bloke falls over or turns to the manager and says "I ain't chasing that." *Joe Kinnear* •762

The problems at Wimbledon seem to be that the club has suffered a loss of complacency.

Joe Kinnear •763

We rode our luck, but that's what the goalposts are there for.

Joe Kinnear •764

Our first goal was pure textile.

John Lambie, legendary '70s manager of Partick Thistle •765

I did once hit a player with a dead pigeon. His name was Declan Roche and he was talking back to me, so I got these dead pigeons out of a box and slapped him with one.
Partick Thistle manager John Lambie •766

The last time we got a penalty away from home, Christ was a carpenter.

Lennie Lawrence suspects a conspiracy against Charlton, 1989 •767

Even when you're dead, you must never allow yourself just to lie down and be buried. *Gordon Lee* •768

I thought my team talk must have lost something in translation when we were a goal down in under a minute and turned round three goals behind.
Palace's Attilio Lombardo on the perils of being a non-English speaking manager •769

179

When people tell me that fans want style and entertainment first I don't believe it. Fans want to win. Style's a bonus.
Lou Macari excuses his tactics as boss at Birmingham •770

Every defeat is a victory in itself.
Colombia manager Francisco Maturana looks on the bright side •771

Yee-hah! I've looked like I've had a coat hanger in my mouth ever since.
Mick McCarthy is clearly delighted to be appointed manager of Sunderland •772

No regrets, none at all. My only regret is that we went out on penalties. That's my only regret. But no, no regrets.
Mick McCarthy is understandably tired and emotional after Ireland go out the 2002 World Cup to Spain •773

Inter have bought the finished article and there's no doubt he can keep improving.
Mick McCarthy •774

If I'd put a number 11 up in the second half they could have all come off.
Mick McCarthy on a poor Wolves performance •775

There's a greyhound going through a field and he sees a rabbit.
The rabbit gets up and starts running. The greyhound fancies a bit
of snap but the rabbit fancies his life. Who runs the hardest? The rabbit.
Mick McCarthy on the eternal chances of the underdog (which, in this instance, isn't the dog) •776

When you've played for a team in Turkey or in a World Cup qualifier in Iran, trust me, you don't get intimidated by Preston.
Mick McCarthy plays down a trip to Deepdale •777

It's been so long since we've had a penalty nobody knew who was taking it. We had forgotten where the spot was.
Middlesbrough manager Steve McClaren bemoans his team's luck •778

When you are 4-0 up, you should never lose 7-1.

Southampton manager Lawrie McMenemy is shell-shocked after a pasting at Watford •779

It's a mixture of feeling sick and wanting to cry at the same time.

Lawrie McMenemy describes the taste of defeat •780

Outside of quality we had other qualities.

Bertie Mee •781

If we lose our passion we might as well end up playing netball.

West Brom manager Gary Megson •782

You lose too many times in this game not to celebrate when you win. *Joe Mercer* •783

Football is war.

Former Holland coach Rinus Michels. **Brilliant Orange** •784

If I wasn't the manager I'd have gone home early.

Hibs manager Alex Miller watches his team's nil-nil •785

Please don't call me arrogant, but I'm European Champion and I think I'm a special one.
José Mourinho on his first press conference as Chelsea manager •786

Young players are a bit like melons. Only when you open and taste the melon are you 100 per cent sure that the melon is good. *José Mourinho* •787

The style of how we play is very important.
But it is omelettes and eggs. No eggs — no omelettes!
It depends on the quality of the eggs. In the supermarket
you have class one, two or class three eggs and some are
more expensive than others and some give you better omelettes.
So when the class one eggs are in Waitrose and you cannot
go there, you have a problem. *José Mourinho* •788

There is no pressure at the top.
The pressure's being second or third.
José Mourinho •789

Does it surprise you he opened
his mouth? You go to a restaurant
sometimes, you know why the fish is
on the table? Because it opened its mouth.

Avram Grant on José Mourinho's departure from Chelsea •790

I am not the Special One –
I am the Normal One.

Avram Grant •791

The run of the ball is
not in our court
at the moment.

Phil Neal •792

I'm not superstitious or anything like that, but I just hope we'll
play our best and put it in the lap of the gods. *Terry Neill* •793

Ian Marshall has been fantastic for us. When he's fit, he's superb. It's just that he's never fit. *Martin O'Neill* •794

I will calm down when I retire or die.
Martin O'Neill refuses to employ his reverse gear •795

I never wanted this bloody job, but it looks like you're stuck with me.
Bob Paisley addresses the Liverpool players for the first time as manager.
He led the club to thirteen major trophies, including three European Cups •796

The last time I drove down here,
I was in a tank liberating Italy.
Bob Paisley in Rome, en route to the 1977 European Cup Final •797

David [Johnson] has scored 62 goals in 148 games for Ipswich and those statistics tell me that he plays games and scores goals. *David Platt* •798

I'm feeling like a drunk who hasn't got a drink. I'd never heard of Groundhog Day until recently but now I must go and see the film.

David Pleat, acting Spurs manager, intoxicated after a 4-4 draw against Leicester that saw his team blow a handsome lead for the second time in a few weeks •799

I cannot tell you what is going to happen tomorrow — only today. And I can not even tell you what is going to happen today.

David Pleat on the precarious existence of being acting manager at Spurs •800

I don't think the fans are too worried whether it's Tom Smith from Bury or Mussolini from Italy… as long as the team's doing well.

David Pleat on Spurs' vacant managerial position •801

I don't think we need foreign managers running the national sides. I've got nothing against foreign managers, they are very nice people. Apart from Arsène Wenger.

Tony Pulis •802

It's 50-50. It's something that, at the moment, is in the fridge.

Real Madrid coach Carlos Queiroz talks gibberish when asked whether Viera would be leaving Arsenal •803

You've won it once, now you've got to win it again.
Sir Alf Ramsey famously exhorts England before extra-time in the 1966
World Cup Final. West Germany had equalised in the last minute •804

Our best football will come against the right type of opposition. A team who come to play football and not act as animals.

Sir Alf Ramsey is incensed by Argentina's tactics during
the 1966 World Cup quarter-final against England •805

There is great harmonium in the dressing room.
Sir Alf Ramsey •806

I suppose I'll have to get used to being called 'sir', but if a player gets formal on the field I will clobber him.
Sir Alf Ramsey on his knighthood, 1967 •807

187

I, Tinkerman, will not change.
Claudio Ranieri delights in his alias •808

In Italy when Chelsea win it is "Chelsea win" or "Abramovich wins" or "Gudjohnsen wins". When Chelsea lose it is "Ranieri loses". But that is normal.
Claudio Ranieri gets paranoid •809

I had to change the team three times between 10.30am and kick-off. I ended up going into the boot room and finding two kids, Anthony Pulis and Warren Hunt, having a cup of tea. I then needed another so I found Shaun Cooper, who was having a meat pie when I told him he was on the bench. *Harry Redknapp despairs at Portsmouth's match-day injury crisis* •810

We'll train Christmas Day. I don't give a shit about Christmas. I'm going to be the most miserable person you have ever seen in your whole life. *Harry Redknapp after Portsmouth's 3-0 defeat at Southampton* •811

He's Australian. He's in the Commonwealth. They fought the war with us. I know that might sound like bollocks to you but we let foreign people in who have no allegiance to this country.
Harry Redknapp goes over the top after Hayden Foxe's work permit gets delayed •813

If you can't pass the bloody ball straight, eating a plateload of pasta ain't going to help.
Harry Redknapp in familiar mode •813

Ramon Vega went down like he was dead. I thought he had broken his leg but he only broke a tie-up.
Harry Redknapp •814

I tape over most of the player videos with Corrie or Neighbours. Most of them are crap. They can fucking make anyone look good. I signed Marco Boogers off a video. He was a good player but a nutter. They didn't show that on the video.
Harry Redknapp •815

In football, if you stand still you go backwards.
Peter Reid •816

I think these foreign coaches have been blown up out of proportion.
Let's see them at Chester, Darlington and Walsall with no money
and see how they get on there. *Peter Reid flies the flag* •817

We threw our dice into the ring
and turned up trumps. *Bruce Rioch* •818

Their keeper played very well and it was not the best
pitch but I am not making excuses. *Graham Rix* •819

The first 90 minutes are the most important. *Bobby Robson* •820

Well, I don't know if I'm going to live to be 127.
*On being asked if he would remain Newcastle's manager
until they won something. Alas he didn't* •821

I'm glad we don't have to play them every week.
Oh, we've got them again on Saturday in the FA Cup.
Bobby Robson after a Newcastle defeat by Arsenal •822

If we starting counting our chickens before they hatch, they won't lay any eggs in the basket.

Bobby Robson •823

Where do you get an experienced player like him with a left foot and a head? *Bobby Robson* •824

That's easy. On Saturday afternoon, Viana; Saturday night, Viagra. *Bobby Robson on selection and scoring* •825

191

We have a one-sided window looking over the players' gym from our physio room. It means we can keep an eye on them…

Bryan Robson on his big-brother managerial style at Middlesbrough •826

We're going to start the game at nil-nil and go out and try and get some goals.

Bryan Robson •827

The ball hit a water sprinkler and shot high in the air. It was purely an instinctive reaction when he grabbed the ball as it flew over his head.

Scotland coach Andy Roxbugh defends Richard Gough's sending-off against Switzerland •828

That was clearly a tackle aimed at getting revenge, or maybe it was just out-and-out retribution.

Joe Royle •829

I've had a good rest, I've had holidays, got to know the wife again, but I've started itching recently.

A between-jobs Joe Royle •830

If that guy was a woman I would be in danger of falling in love with him.
Bill Shankly is impressed by Muhammad Ali •831

There's only two teams in Liverpool; Liverpool and Liverpool reserves.

Bill Shankly •832

Some people think football is a matter of life and death. I don't like that attitude. I can assure them it is much more serious than that.
The oft-misquoted Bill Shankly •833

Professional footballers should have more sense than to consider marrying during the season. Anybody who does isn't behaving professionally as far as I'm concerned.
Bill Shankly •834

There are nil-nils and nil-nils, and this was nil-nil. *John Sillett* •835

Statistics are like miniskirts. They give you good ideas but hide the most important things.

Hibs manager Ebbe Skovdahl •836

Today's top players only want to play in London or for Manchester United. That's what happened when I tried to sign Alan Shearer and he went to Blackburn. *Graeme Souness* •837

Clearly, Graeme, it all went according to plan. What was the plan exactly?

Souness's tactics prove too cunning for Elton Welsby •838

We should be going home wearing pointed hats with the word 'dopes' written on them. *Graeme Souness reacts badly to a Blackburn defeat at Upton Park* •839

John, you're immortal.

Bill Shankly to Jock Stein after Celtic's 1967 European Cup triumph •840

We'll try and win because we're not clever enough to try anything else.
Gordon Strachan before Southampton's UEFA Cup tie against Steaua Bucharest •841

You could smell the fear in my players in the first 45 minutes — I've never seen that before, no matter who we've played. We've always had the stomach for the fight, but it wasn't there. You can't live life with fear like that, never mind football.
Gordon Strachan condemns his Southampton team's approach against Arsenal •842

Apart from yourself, we're all quite positive round here. I'm going to whack you over the head with a big stick. Down, negative man, down.
Gordon Strachan to another hapless reporter •843

No, I'm just going to crumble like a wreck. I'll go home, become an alcoholic and maybe jump off a bridge.
Gordon Strachan on being asked whether he could take the pressure •844

I don't know. I'll have to see where Easyjet are going.

Gordon Strachan's travel plans remained hazy following his departure from St. Mary's •845

Minging.

Gordon Strachan (Southampton manager)
with his verdict on Bolton 0-0 Southampton •846

You're right. It is a daft question. I'm not even going to bother answering that one. You're spot on there.

Gordon Strachan with another press conference classic •847

I just panicked.

Graham Taylor's explanation for signing Ian Ormondroyd for Aston Villa •848

To be really happy, we must throw our hearts over the bar and hope that our bodies will follow. *Graham Taylor •849*

Shearer could be at 100% fitness but not peak fitness. *Graham Taylor •850*

It's the only way we can lose, irrespective of the result.

Graham Taylor •851

I'd never allow myself to let myself call myself a coward. *Graham Taylor •852*

My wife isn't talking to me. She blames me for what happened. My son Andy drove me home on Sunday night and isn't talking to me either. I'd left him out of the team and there was nothing he could do to save us. *Bolton manager Colin Todd after the team's relegation from the Premiership •853*

We can't behave like crocodiles and cry over spilled milk and broken eggs. *Then Italy coach Giovanni Trappatoni loses it in translation •854*

A lot of people seem to think I'm a slippery cockney boy with a few jokes. It has taken one of the biggest clubs in the world to acknowledge what I can really do — coach. *Terry Venables on his managership of Barcelona* •855

There are two ways of getting the ball. One is from your team-mates and that's the only way.

Terry Venables •856

The mere fact that he's injured stops him getting injured again, if you know what I mean.
Terry Venables •857

Those are the sort of doors that get opened if you don't close them.

Terry Venables •858

For the first time I'm at a club where I believe I've got a chance to win it.
Terry Venables on his appointment as manager of Leeds. They finished 15th; Venables failed to finish the season •859

Our coach driver thinks he's Ben Hur, so I see prayer as an alternative to brakes.

Congo national coach Mick Wadsworth on the reason for his leading prayer sessions at training •860

I just wonder what would have happened if the shirt had been on the other foot. *Mike Walker* •861

We have to improve in two key areas: defence and attack.

Belgium national coach Robert Waseige on his team's performance in Euro 2000 •862

A football team is like a beautiful woman. When you do not tell her so, she forgets to be beautiful.

Arsène Wenger •863

Davor has a left leg and a nose in the box.

Arsène Wenger on the anatomy of striker Davor Suker •864

Out of nine red cards this season we probably deserved half of them.

Arsène Wenger •865

Why don't they put us in Division One?

Arsène Wenger gets a complex as Arsenal's disciplinary record comes up before the FA... again •866

200

We have to roll up our sleeves and get our knees dirty.

Howard Wilkinson •867

You can't give a team confidence.
You can't put it in a pill, or a suppository.

Howard Wilkinson tries to explain Sunderland's capitulation in the Premier League •868

There was nothing between the teams apart from seven goals.

Barnsley boss Danny Wilson has tongue in cheek after a mauling at Old Trafford •869

We have faced African teams, we have faced English teams – so we are ready to face Scotland because we know what their play will be like.

Brazilian coach Mario Zagallo flunks the geography test before the 1998 World Cup curtain-raiser against Scotland •870

Boardroom Bollocks

At home they have a few drinks and probably the prawn sandwiches, and they don't realise what's going on out on the pitch. I don't think some of the people who come to Old Trafford can spell football, never mind understand it.
Roy Keane •871

Of course I am prepared to bury the hatchet – right in the back of Sam Longson's head.
Brian Clough on not kissing and making up with his former chairman at Derby •872

We haven't fallen out. You can't fall out with somebody you never talk to.
Keegan on Newcastle chairman Sir John Hall •873

I'd like to thank Stan for his interest but we won't be taking it seriously.
Chairman Geoffrey Richmond politely declines Stan Collymore's application to become Bradford City's manager •874

The only reason David won't be manager of Leeds will be if he walks out because he and I are in this together.
Peter Ridsdale, Leeds chairman, six weeks before sacking O'Leary •875

In many ways he's an absolute ignorant pig, but he does care about the club.
Barnet manager Barry Fry on Stan Flashman, the club's ticket-touting chairman •876

He couldn't run a kebab shop.
Millwall chairman Theo Paphitis on Football League chief executive David Burns •877

We spoke about it really and out of it came the fact that we wouldn't speak about it.
Terry Venables on discussions about his future with Middlesbrough chairman Steve Gibson •878

We will not miss him. He can't head the ball and he rarely passes the ball more than three metres. *Real Madrid president, Florentino Perez, as Claude Makélélé departs for Stamford Bridge* •879

They want us to be a nodding dog in the back of their car. *The PFA's Gordon Taylor bemoans the attitude of the Premier League* •880

I will close Hull City down if I don't get proper backing from the club and supporters, and those who don't like it can get stuffed. *Proprietor David Lloyd* •881

I don't believe evil should triumph and he was an evil man. I did not grieve because I am not a hypocrite… he was full of bullshit, star-struck and up Glenn Hoddle's arse.
Chelsea chairman Ken Bates reflects on director Matthew Harding's fatal helicopter crash •882

Get lost, Abramovich. I think I speak for the rest of football. *Charlton chairman Martin Simons is peeved about Chelsea's interest in Scott Parker* •883

Our only regret is that Jack Walker invested in Blackburn, not us. *Darwen's chairwoman Kath Marah* •884

The great thing about local rivalries is that when things are going pear-shaped, you can have a go at your neighbour. Step forward our good friends at Crippled Alice who took umbrage with our decision to part company with Mark. *Millwall chairman Theo Paphitis blasts Crystal Palace after they criticised their rival's sacking of manager Mark McGhee* •885

I'd rather die and have vultures eat my insides than share with Crystal Palace. *Wimbledon chairman Sam Hammam* •886

There's a village somewhere that's missing a fool. *Paphitis again, this time slating Burnley boss Stan Ternent after claims of racism by Millwall fans* •887

The ideal soccer board of directors should be made up of three men; two dead, and the other dying. *Tommy Docherty* •888

I can remember who was ready to whisper in an ear or two for their own ends. Now Vialli has found out that what goes round, comes round. *Ruud Gullit on Vialli's sacking at Chelsea* •889

I have flown economy and haven't had a problem with it. It's good discipline.

Chairman Peter Hill-Wood relegates Arsenal's players after a pre-season trip to Austria •890

Soccer is like vodka ten years ago. The public's going to have to be educated to it.

W.B Cutler, US soccer club chairman, on his plans to market the game in the States •891

The supporters don't matter as far as I'm concerned. They just pay their entrance fee. I don't care whether they come to Barnet or not... *The late Barnet chairman, Stan Flashman* •892

If a Russian billionaire came in I would not only roll out the red carpet but I would hoist up the red flag. *Bob Murray, Sunderland chairman* •893

In a fairly dull kingdom there were two players who were perfectly happy, because they had firm contracts. However, due to a shortage of beans, the two players were dispatched to far-flung kingdoms to ply their trade with other clubs.
Start of programme notes from QPR chairman David Davies, February 2004 •894

They go in because they are football crazy, or football mad. You have to be bloody crackers to be a director of a football club anyway. Who'd pour money into football when you can earn 10% with it, maybe 20% with it? *Ex-Palace chairman Arthur Wait* •895

OK, they cost us £20 a month to hire, but they were in the club colours of blue and yellow.
Peter Ridsdale justifies the hire of tropical fish to decorate his office •896

That's a matter between directors and club. Listen, lad, I wouldn't even tell the wife. *Stafford Heginbotham, ex-Bradford City chairman, on how much he had invested* •897

A message for the best football supporters in the world: We need a 12th man here. Where are you? Where are you? Let's be having you!

Delia Smith's now legendary half-time call-to-arms to the Norwich fans •898

It's like pushing water up a hill.

Delia Smith on the effort of exhorting Norwich City to better things •899

I'm delighted for Claudio Ranieri that we beat Fulham in the FA Cup semi-final, as if we'd lost yesterday, it would have been a pity to sack him just after he'd signed a new contract.

Ken Bates dispenses with the vote of confidence •900

Supporters, shareholders, the press, the manager, nobody was saying don't do it.

Peter Ridsdale passes the buck for Leeds' financial fall from grace •901

The first thing I read now in the *Telegraph* is the obituaries. If I'm not in it, I have a good day.

Wolves chairman Jack Hayward looks on the bright side of life •902

I'd like to finish on page one of Ceefax.

Chairman Jack Hayward on Wolves Premiership ambitions, August 2003 •903

Every fan you ask will say he wants to see lively, open football. But what the fan really wants to see is his team win.

Dennis Hill-Wood, Arsenal director •904

I haven't felt this bad since I killed a man.

Uri Geller, Exeter director and former Israeli soldier, on his team's relegation to the Conference •905

Sacking a manager is as big an event in my life as drinking a glass of beer. I'd hire twenty managers a year if I wanted to, 100 if necessary. *President of Atletico Madrid, Jesús Gil* •906

Cardiff are a substantially bigger club than Leeds.

Chairman Sam Hamman pours oil before an FA Cup Tie •907

I have a clear message to Sir Alex and anyone else who is interested: "read my lips, Louis Saha is not for sale."

Fulham chairman Mohammed Al Fayed lays it on the line, 6th January 2004, a couple of weeks before Saha left for Old Trafford •908

In ten years' time this club will be in the Premier League.
Michael Knighton in 1992, on buying Carlisle United.
They dropped into the Conference in 2004 •909

Newcastle girls are all dogs. England is full of them.

Newcastle director Freddie Shepherd unwittingly spills the beans to an undercover tabloid hack •910

Shearer's boring. We call him Mary Poppins. He never gets into trouble.

Freddie Shepherd... again... to the same journalist •911

Our fans like people like Keith Gillespie – they relate to people who like to have a drink and get into trouble.

Newcastle chairman Douglas Hall •912

We have made an undertaking to Arsène Wenger and his family not to name our new coach.

Arsenal chairman Peter Hill-Wood •913

Tell the Kraut to get his ass up front. We don't pay a million for a guy to hang around in defence.

A New York Cosmos executive questions Franz Beckenbauer's position •914

If they had listened to me the supporters would be sitting in a 70,000-seater stadium in Dublin and in the Premiership.

Former Wimbledon boss Joe Kinnear — they ended up in the hockey stadium in Milton Keynes, capacity 6,000 •915

My job will be to make sure that he scores more goals than own goals.

Publicist Max Clifford on his new client, Mohammed Al Fayed •916

The rumours are all driving us mad. Paul is staying with us. I wish people would leave it alone. Paul's totally committed to the club.
Plymouth chairman Paul Stapleton, two days before manager Paul Sturrock left for Southampton •917

I didn't buy Manchester United so why should I buy Arsenal? We'll thrash them all at the Manor.
The late, largely unloved Robert Maxwell blusters about Oxford United •918

Me and Joe are so close, we will continue living in the same underpants.
Ex-Wimbledon chairman Sam Hammam talks pants about his former manager, Joe Kinnear •919

I'm leaving the asylum to the lunatics. *Keith Harris ends his tenure as Football League chairman* •920

If I had a son I'd prefer he went to war than play soccer. There are terrible battles in soccer, worse than war itself. *Real Madrid president Santiago Bernabeu, 1964 •921*

It is the board's view that in spite of recent results, the team's performance has failed to live up to the high standard of football entertainment expected of Manchester United.
Statement from Manchester United dismissing manager Dave Sexton in 1981. The team has just won its seventh game in a row •922

Maxwell Chairman? We may as well have Max Wall. *Derby fanzine The Sheep •923*

Once it was lucky Arsenal. Then it was boring Arsenal, but now we've got a real problem because we're in danger of being liked. *Arsenal chairman Peter Hill-Wood on the flair of late '90s Arsenal •924*

As we say in the Conference, they didn't like it when we got inside their pants. I've never seen Shearer out of his pram like that. He didn't like it when we wouldn't let them play.

Victor Green, Stevenage chairman, after holding Newcastle in an FA Cup tie •925

It takes one to know one. I'm surprised Martin O'Neill knows as big a word as cretin.

Ken Bates goes back to the playground •926

If I had to choose between the Israelis or Tony Blair to protect me, then Israel wins every time.

Ken Bates remains unimpressed by some Chelsea players'
refusal to fly to Tel Aviv for a UEFA Cup Tie •927

I have a gun and a licence and I wouldn't mind blowing their brains out.

Nuremberg president Adolf Roth reacts badly to his team's 2-1 defeat to Lubeck •928

Never, never, never, never.
Nothing, never, never, never.
Not now. Not ever.

*Real Madrid president, Florentino Perez, on
whether the club would sign David Beckham* •929

Carreras, Santi and Otero are no good. They can die.
I mean it: some of the players don't deserve to live.

Atletico Madrid president Jesús Gil •930

A piece of bread, and a very sensitive one.

Self-portrait by Atletico Madrid supremo Jesús Gil •931

There is a psychological value… you can imagine
when the players of an opposition team go out
knowing that Darth Vader is watching them.

*Exeter chairman Uri Geller reacting to Dave Prowse
becoming an honorary director* •932

I liken the current situation to that of the Starship Enterprise.
The shields are up and the Klingons are shooting at us and
every time they land a punch they are sapping our power…

*Southampton chairman Rupert Lowe proves Gordon Strachan
wasn't the only eccentric at St. Mary's* •933

You should see his boots. They're like something you hang from your car mirror. *Middlesbrough chairman Steve Gibson marvels at the size of Juninho's feet •934*

I've often looked at other people getting involved in games like that and thought 'What a prat'. Perhaps I enjoyed it a little more than I should have but I was wrapped up in the occasion.

Middlesbrough chairman Steve Gibson after celebrating his club's first major trophy, the Carling Cup, in 2004 •935

I've got a gut feeling in my stomach…

Alan Sugar passes his anatomy test •936

I parted on good terms with Luca Vialli. As he left the room and I led him to the door, we departed with the usual Italian formalities of a bear-hug and a kiss. *Ken Bates attempts to prove that not everybody hated him •937*

I can't ever leave this club. I was born 300 yards from Molineux. The only way I'll leave this place is in a coffin. *Jack Hayward declares undying allegiance to Wolves •938*

Even Jesus Christ suffered only one Pontius Pilate.
I had a whole team of them.

*Ken Bates resigns in a huff from the company
contracted to rebuild Wembley* •939

He has left the Theatre of Dreams for the Team of Dreams.

Real Madrid president Florentino Perez welcomes David Beckham •940

The World Cup, believe it or not, was brought to my house and I held it in my hands and closed my eyes, and I energized it for England. To be very honest with you, I even managed to bend it ever so slightly.

Uri Geller. Course you did, Uri •941

Win or die.

*Mussolini's pre-match telegram before the 1938 World Cup Final had the desired effect.
Italy won* •942

Lombardo speaks much better English than what people realise.

Ex-Palace chairman Mark Goldberg •943

Fees, FIFA and Filthy Lucre

Let the women play in more feminine clothes, like they do in volleyball. They could, for example, have tighter shorts. Female players are pretty, if you excuse me for saying so... *FIFA president Sepp Blatter* •944

I think in football there is too much modern slavery, transferring players or buying players here and there, and putting them somewhere.

Sepp Blatter. But, Sepp, they get paid a fortune and slaves... Oh, never mind •945

I read the letter. I don't think the players wrote it. It was typed out on a computer and there were no spelling mistakes.
FFF Gen Sec Henri Monteil on the French World Cup ruccus •946

When UEFA get in their stride, they make the FA look like kindergarten material.
Brian Clough •947

There is a mafia even in the soccer world. The penalty didn't exist. It was given to let the Germans win.
Diego Maradona spits sour grapes after the 1990 World Cup Final •948

People have been making money out of me.
Don Revie answers criticism of greed, after he left England to take a
coaching job in Saudi Arabia •949

We are standing in a one-way alley with bullets flying all around us.
John Smith, co-chairman at Bury, spells out his club's
financial position •950

If it is a case of losing 10,000 season tickets versus the £9m we have just generated from Jonathan Woodgate, there is no discussion.
Leeds chairman Peter Ridsdale endears himself to supporters...not •951

He has been very well paid for his time at the club. It's not as if he's going to end up in a bedsit in Gipton.
Simon Jose, co-founder of Leeds United Independent Fans' Association,
on Peter Ridsdale •952

It wasn't the Leeds thing to do at all. Leeds is built on good, solid Jewish money. And a lot of good, solid Jewish people are lamenting what Peter Ridsdale did.
Leeds local Martin Pickles •953

To be perfectly blunt, the introduction of the Bosman ruling was a disaster for sport and especially for football.

Gerhard Aigner, former UEFA chief executive •954

With Ravanelli and Emerson, perhaps their brains really were in their boots and their hearts in their wallets. *Middlesbrough chairman Steve Gibson* •955

I have spent some time with some tough cookies over the years, Mrs Thatcher and Saddam Hussein to name but two. But when it comes to ruthlessness in defence of his own interests, Ken Bates leaves them all behind. *David Mellor* •956

I raised the matter [of top-rate season tickets at £1,000] with Ken Bates the other day. He just replied "You can afford it". This attitude is becoming all too evident in football.

Tony Banks, Chelsea fan and ex-Minister for Sport •957

The listening bank refused to listen and the bank which likes to say yes said no.

Hartlepool chairman Garry Gibson contemplates a winding-up order from the inland revenue •958

The local pubs aren't happy that there's 25,000 and not 48,000 in the ground. And then there's the nearby strip club and the strippers aren't too happy either. It's bad for top totty and the lap-dancing club has closed.
Sunderland chairman Bob Murray laments the post-relegation recession •959

I think what's going on is sad and disappointing because everyone that's helped give the club history and tradition is being sold down the river.
Ex-Wimbledon hero Dave Beasant laments the current state of the Dons •960

I've had enough. As soon as I get home, I'm going to buy that club. I'm going to walk in and say "You, fuck off. You, fuck off. You, make me a cup of tea. You, fuck off.

Noel Gallagher muses whether the Oasis school of diplomacy will work at Manchester City •961

You can spend £2m and find the player can not trap the ball.

Graham Taylor on the inflated transfer market, 2001 •962

It is not easy to change a culture in which people are used to hiding things. They might not have anything to hide but the tendency is to secrecy.

Kate Barker, chair of the the FA's Finance Advisory Committee, February 2004 •963

The only thing that put me on the right path was the realisation that I could now earn big money and I liked that idea.

Jack Charlton on his late improvement as a player, 1965 •964

There's a prosperous sound about twenty pounds a week. It rolls off the tongue, but it doesn't roll into the pockets of every player.

Brian Clough, 1958 •965

I believe that the introduction of big money to English football has had side effects. There is more violence. But these problems, which arise out of the new professional attitude of the players, are rather like those of the spirited young horse which needs controlling firmly.

Jimmy Hill reflects on the abolition of the maximum wage, 1967 •966

We needed someone with deeper pockets than I've got.

Ken Bates recognises the buying power of new owner Roman Abramovich •967

Roman Abramovich has parked his Russian tank in our front garden and is firing £50 notes at us.

Arsenal director David Dein gets envious •968

It makes the house that Jack built at Blackburn look like a bungalow.

Henk Potts, financial analyst, on Roman Abramovich's spending at Chelsea •969

Everybody wants to speak to me now I've got money.

Ken Bates on the power of Abramovich •970

We have to wait for others to shake the apples from the tree, then try to make sure we are in a position to react quickly to the apples left on the ground.

Tony Pulis on the less wealthy clubs fighting for scraps in the transfer market •971

We lived the dream.

Ex-Leeds chairman Peter Ridsdale, who left the club £80m in debt •972

It's like an oil tanker that's heading for the rocks… the trouble with oil tankers is they're two miles long and they don't turn round in two minutes.

Leeds chairman John McKenzie on picking up the financial pieces at Elland Road •973

Why leave a club that is two quid in debt and go to a club that is £80m in debt?

Norwich manager Nigel Worthington dismisses talk that he is bound for Leeds •974

Celtic's support is the greatest asset…
when you start talking about money, it is
the supporters that put the money into
the club. *Martin O'Neill points out where the real wealth lies* •975

Only two clubs could buy him:
Real Madrid and Chelsea.
Everton manager David Moyes values Wayne Rooney •976

I can understand him being a little sad because his team were
clearly dominated by a team who have maybe 10% of his budget.
*Porto coach José Mourinho digs after Alex Ferguson refused to shake hands after
United's Champions League defeat* •977

Two months ago he was over
the moon, now he's asking for it.
Juventus' official with his own take on Paolo Rossi's pay demands •978

I cannot feed my child on glory.
Paolo Rossi during his pay dispute with Juventus •979

Any small boy, anyone who kicks a ball owns a piece of the action. Everybody enjoys the exaggeration and romance of a sporting story, but deliberate lying and cheating for profit is something else.

Danny Blanchflower, speaking in 1968, on power, corruption and money •980

I've still one or two ambitions left. Number one is to make £50,000 by the time I'm 25, and number two is to own a chain of shops and, who knows, eventually to become a millionaire.

George Best maps out the future, 1967 •981

We bring in the crowds, it's an entertainment, and we're vastly underpaid, footballers, for the entertainment we provide. *Stan Bowles* •982

These so-called stars are people we are supposed to be looking up to. Well they are weak and soft. If they don't want to come because their wife wants to go shopping in London, it's a sad state of affairs.

Roy Keane gets all antsy about big names' unwillingness to go to Sunderland •983

Just because you are paid £120,000 a week and play well for 20 minutes against Tottenham, you think you are a superstar.

Roy Keane lays it on the line to Rio Ferdinand. To be fair Ferdinand upped his game •984

In Madrid it was easy because I lived in a hotel. The bell boy's job was to bring me three pastries after sex. He would hand me the pastries, I would hand him the girl, and he'd return her into the night. Sex plus pastries — could it be any better.
Antonio Cassano of Sampdoria and Italy from maybe the most crass football autobiography yet published, Dico Tutto •985

I love Bradford, the fans and the palyers — and they love me. We're one big family. When I signed for Bradford it was for four years and I want to stay until my contract finishes. I will respect it. *Benito Carbone, 2002, four days before leaving for Middlesbrough* •986

Money comes in at the top end and goes straight to the players. Then, when a player leaves, he'll blame the club and say he's sorry to go because he loves the place. Well it's crap. They want to move for a better deal and more money. It's just greed. On his way out, the player will probably ask for a loyalty bonus. *Dave Bassett enjoys a rant* •987

I, who have had the most privileged of lives, the most carefree of existences for nearly twenty years, have managed to get myself painted as a living saint for keeping my promise to myself.

Niall Quinn's take, in his autobiography, on his donation of a £1m testimonial gate to charity •988

The whole problem with football players is they really take themselves seriously. We kick a ball around and we earn 100,000, 200,000 or even 300,000 euros a week. We don't improve the world. It's not like we invented hot water.

Tottenham's Benoît Assou-Ekoto keeps his feet on the ground •989

When my career ends, I cannot go the baker and say "I'm Johan Cruyff, give me some bread".

Cruyff on the need to keep earning bread •990

They sold me like a cow.

Jaap Stam bears a grudge after leaving Manchester United for Lazio •991

When I was a lad, I took nothing for granted,
the air I breathed or even a scrap of bread.
Now you can offer a boy the world and
he'll probably turn his nose up.

Bill Shankly despairs of the nation's youth •992

Listen, for the next three years while I am in Spain, I am
not a man. I am not a football player. I am an industry.

Johan Cruyff after signing a $1m contract with Barcelona, 1973 •993

There was always a
lot of talk of money,
but I still play 95% for
the joy of the game.

Johan Cruyff •994

I don't know how
much it is. My father
told me that when you're
working, don't stop to
count your money.

*Pele in 1974, on being asked
how much he was worth* •995

Yeah. I have been offered money to sign somebody and
there's not a manager in the country who would tell you
different. If they did they'd be lying. *Harry Redknapp* •996

These agents get you over to see this fantastic striker you can take on loan, you get there and he's on the bench. On Friday I'm stood outside a hotel in Alaves at four o'clock in the morning, pissing down with rain… I thought to myself "I wonder if Arsène Wenger or Alex Ferguson would be stood outside this hotel at 4am in Alaves? What am I doing?"
Harry Redknapp on his desperate search for a new striker in his pre-Tottenham days •997

It's costing me a fortune, because as well as the fares I'm arriving late for training a few times. We have a deal where anyone who is late has to pay £50, so I've already written a cheque for £1,500 to see me through the season.
Paul Merson on playing for Middlesbrough and living in Hertfordshire •998

Don't know much about the game. Don't even like it much. What's that got to do with it? My business is selling people – makes no difference what they do.
Players' agent Eric Hall reveals his true love •999

The terrible thing about my job is that players get 80% of my earnings.
Agent Eric Hall inflates his importance... again •1000

It may be good enough for the homeless but not for an international striker.

Pierre van Hooijdonk's rejection of a £7,000 per week pay rise •1001

Football is a street where every second building is a last-chance saloon.

The Sunday Times' *David Walsh waxes all lyrical* •1002

When you look at other sports, like golf, the players earn a lot more money without running around. I wish I had that little cart to take me to the corner kicks.

Thierry Henry •1003

Pulling down your shorts on a football field is
a) against our regulations because it is ungentlemanly conduct, and
b) it is also against the FIFA regulation which stipulates that footballers are barred from using their bodies or undergarments beneath their kit as advertisement boards. *FA spokesman Adrian Bevington warns Scarborough players not to exploit too many commercial opportunities during their FA Cup tie against Chelsea* •1004

Football in the 1970s is very rewarding financially and can provide the opportunity to travel to almost any country in the world.

Don Revie, shortly before walking out of the England job to take up a lucrative coaching post in Saudi Arabia •1005

Some people tell me that we professional players are soccer slaves. Well, if this is slavery, give me a life sentence.

Bobby Charlton on the maximum wage, 1960 •1006

If I never kicked another ball I could afford to live well for the rest of my life. It is a comforting thought for a man only twenty-four years old.

Pele in 1965 •1007

I can play football at my level for £500 a month, because I love it so much.

Marcel Desailly has his fingers crossed, 2003 •1008

Players who play to lose are worse than bank robbers.
Bill Shankly •1009

The whole problem with Hillsborough seems to be it was the fans who suffered and died and they haven't got any benefits out of Hillsborough at all, and so many other people have.
Sheila Spiers of the Football Supporters' Association •1010

He spat on Russia by buying Chelsea. He abandoned our teams which need support.
Mayor of Moscow Yuri Lushnov on Roman Abramovich •1011

Any soccer club that pays income tax at the end its financial year, I would fine them exactly the same amounts on the grounds that they were guilty of bad management. Soccer can not afford to lose a penny that comes into the game, let alone pay it out in income tax. *Brian Clough, 1973* •1012

I believe Wembley is the next Millennium Dome. There will be a lot of tears if they continue this project. *Ex Aston Villa Chairman Doug Ellis* •1013

I'm going to have to listen for offers for all my players – and the club cat, Benny, who is pissed off because there are no mice to catch because they have all died of starvation. *John McGrath, Halifax manager, in 1992* •1014

How can you sympathise with a club which had a perfectly good stadium seven years ago but sold it to Toys R Us? *Brighton fan Paul Millmore* •1015

240

Northampton are currently making payments to four managers but not paying any bills.

Terry Fenwick comments on a 48-day tenure as the Cobblers' manager •1016

I'm aware of the situation.
There's not £10m to spend.
There's not even 10p.

Tony Adams's verdict on Wycombe's finances •1017

I am here to earn big money at Tottenham and to meet English girls.

Spurs' new signing Moussa Saib sets out his priorities •1018

If I wanted to sign a Madrid player my first call would be to the club, not the newspapers. I expect a bit more class from Real Madrid.

Arsène Wenger, after Real's interest in Thierry Henry is made public •1019

It spends money it hasn't got on players who aren't worth it. What kind of business is that? A bankrupt one is the answer.

Michael Parkinson despairs of football's finances •1020

Down Among
The Dead Men

There's an old joke in football about the manager of a Fourth Division club, pushing out his humble team for a cup match against a big First Division club. 'Go out there lads and do your best' he exhorts them, 'so I can get enough money to replace you'.

Hunter Davies, from seminal football book **The Glory Game** •1021

I enjoyed myself playing for Scunthorpe – what more could you ask for? *Kevin Keegan* •1022

Plenty of goals in Divisions Three and Four today; Darlington nil, Hereford nil.

BBC Radio 2 announcer •1023

Brentford reserves were involved in a nine-goal thriller when they beat Orient 4-3.

Match report in the **Ealing Gazette** •1024

We learned a lot from United today, including how to count.

Shrewsbury boss Kevin Ratcliffe laments an 8-1 pre-season hammering by Manchester United •1025

244

Chesterfield 1 Chester 1 — another score draw in the local derby.
Des Lynam •1026

It's now 4–3 to Oldham, the goals are going in like dominoes.
Over-excited report from Manchester's Piccadilly Radio •1027

Since his arrival from West Ham, Michael Hughes' impact, like an elephant catapulted at an ant, has been considerable. *Wimbledon's programme notes* •1028

When you're down, you Palace fans, the fickle finger of fate rarely smiles on you.
Jonathan Pearce •1029

I set aside everything I learned under Arsène Wenger. It's a complete waste of time at this level. They just can't take a lot of information on board. *Wycombe manager Tony Adams questions the tactical nous of his team* •1030

Some of our players have got no brains, so I've given them the day off tomorrow to rest them.
Oxford's Dave Kemp •1031

That's one game over and 45 headaches to come.

Stoke manager Steve Cotterill after the opening day of the season •1032

We were woeful and I am embarrassed to be their manager.

Burnley boss Stan Ternent after a 3-0 defeat puts the Clarets bottom of Division One •1033

Last week's match was a real game of cat and dog.

Tranmere boss John Aldridge •1034

Dave has this incredible knack of pulling a couple of chickens out of the hat each season. *Mark McGhee* •1035

We attacked like Real Madrid but defended like a team from the Dog and Duck.

Huddersfield manager Mick Wadsworth after a 3-3 draw with Cheltenham Town •1036

As a striker, you are either in a purple patch or struggling. At the moment, I'm somewhere in between. *Bob Taylor* •1037

They're bound to finish bottom unless there's a place even lower in the bloody table.
Peter Taylor on first surveying the scene at Hartlepool •1038

We're getting Port Vale into the First Division. One at a time!
Stoke boss Ritchie Barker on signing three Port Vale players in as many months •1039

They're aren't many jock-straps to be found in our dressing-room, only nappies.

Wrexham manager Brian Flynn on his emphasis on youth •1040

I've been at Port Vale for 16 years. Even the Great Train Robbers didn't get that long a sentence. Here you are manager, coach, chief scout, chief cook and bottle washer, but I've loved every minute of it. *John Rudge* •1041

…after winning the Second Division championship we expected to settle down comfortably in our rightful place of mid-table mediocrity and expectations were low. Apart, of course, from the sort of people who queue up every week to wait for the turnstiles to open, dribble when they talk, and wear the entire contents of the club shop. *Paul Gillman from Millwall's* **The Lion Roars** *fanzine* •1042

There were no hiding places out there, and I had players putting their family jewels in front of the ball.

Manager Danny Wilson in praise of his Bristol City boys •1043

I don't know what it's like out there, but it's like an ice rink out there.

Stockport manager Andy Kilner •1044

For me to take the manager of the month award, I would have to win nine games out of eight.

Sheffield United's Neil Warnock •1045

It would be foolish to believe that automatic promotion is automatic in any way whatsoever. *Dave Bassett* •1046

They'll be dancing in the streets of Raith tonight. *David Coleman fails to grasp that Raith Rovers play in Kircaldy* •1047

The boys' feet have been up in the clouds since the win.
Alan Buckley •1048

It looks as if I am trying to stab Dave Bassett in the
back but I'm not holding a gun to anybody's head.
Micky Adams •1049

We ended up playing football and that doesn't suit our style.

Frank admission from Airdrie manager Alex MacDonald •1050

He's a tree surgeon who once had to have his arm sewn
back on, so facing Thierry Henry won't faze him.
Farnborough manager Graham Westley on defender Nathan Bunce,
after drawing Arsenal in the FA Cup •1051

They used to boo me before we'd even kicked off –
"Number seven Nicky Summerbee" and they all booed.
That's great for your confidence, isn't it?
Nicky Summerbee on failing to win over the Maine Road faithful •1052

If you go shopping at Sainsbury's and ask for a fillet steak but can't afford it, you have to find something else and we've ended up with a gristly old fatty lump of lard up front – but it tasted good.

Manager Martin Allen of Cheltenham pays Julian Allsop a back-handed compliment after resigning him in 2009 •1053

The back four were like powder-puff girls, like the Tiller Girls. *Rotherham's Ronnie Moore is unhappy with commitment levels at Millmoor •1054*

Managing is a seven-day-a-week, almost 24-hour a day job. There's no rest and no escape, but I'm hooked on it. *Barry Fry •1055*

It's a great job during the week, but sometimes the Saturday spoils it. *Southport manager Mike Walsh •1056*

It's a great job apart from Saturday afternoons.

Jocky Scott on the manager's job at Dunfermline •1057

It will take a very, very long time to sort things out. It is a rat-infested place.
Outgoing City manager Frank Clark on the problems at Maine Road •1058

We are the ailing patient. We moved to Milton Keynes to get over a serious illness, and now we are on a life-support with our organs removed, waiting for a miracle. *Wimbledon manager Stuart Murdoch finds that the 2003/04 season is about to die on him* •1059

I could do a better job than Vialli at Chelsea… sadly, people like me are not the in-thing right now. You need to be Italian, wear sunglasses, drive a beautiful car and know all about the beautiful game.
The then Notts County boss Sam Allardyce shows he's not bitter •1060

Being manager of Barnet was like living with a double-decker bus on your head. When I left it was like it had been driven off.
Barry Fry lets his job get on top of him •1061

A failed football club in October. A depressing place. Already, with seven months to go, the morning becomes a dread. *Eamon Dunphy describes Millwall in 1973* •1067

The place is like a morgue. Most of those that did come are moaning bastards. There's no home advantage for us.
Wimbledon manager Joe Kinnear bemoans another tiny attendance at Selhurst Park •1063

Sunderland fans came to my door crying, something which had never happened before. Three generations of the one family came and left again, all of them crying. They just turned and went, never saw them before or since.
Niall Quinn recalls grief in Sunderland after a lost penalty shoot-out denied the Maccams a place in the Premiership •1064

When I said even my Missus could save Derby from relegation, I was exaggerating.
Peter Taylor, ex-Cloughie sidekick •1065

I may be desperate but I'm not that desperate.
Middlesbrough's Dean Windass after refusing to join his father-in-law's team,
North Ferriby United •1066

Although we are playing Russian roulette, we are obviously playing Catch 22
at the moment and that's a difficult scenario to get my head round.
Paul Sturrock •1067

I left as I arrived –
fired with enthusiasm.

John McGrath on getting the bullet from Preston •1068

There were ten of us who used to hang around together in Streatham.
At the last count, only two of us were on the outside [of prison].
Football was my way out and that was my fortune.
Phil Babb reflects on his escape •1069

How could you finish your life as a sparky knowing that you could have been a professional footballer? What's security when you're 21, single, living with your parents and paying your mum £30 a week?

Stuart Pearce on the moment he swapped an electrician's apprenticeship and a part-time contract at Wealdstone for Coventry City •1070

There are only two fucking toilets, and they've run out of pies, coffee, fucking everything. This is the worst ground I've ever been to in my fucking life.

Layer Road, Colchester, gets the thumbs-down from a Manchester City fan •1071

A 21st century stadium, with 14th century stewarding. *An away fan's view of Home Park, Plymouth.* •1072

We were miles adrift at the bottom, our disciplinary record had seen us tot up more points than Johnny Logan in Eurovision, and through it all our tactics had become as predictable as Harry Potter at the box office.

Y3KShakers.com, a Bury website •1073

Jesus turned water into wine. Kemp is turning Oxford into Accrington Stanley.

Disgruntled Oxford fan Julia Toogood. It wasn't meant literally, but by a twist of fate Oxford were soon out of the league and Stanley had regained their league status •1074

Coventry are the untouched bottle of Lea & Perrin's sauce at the back of the kitchen cupboard. Coventry are the pair of socks you meant to chuck out ages ago but have survived in the bottom drawer against all odds. *Dave Cottrell in 90 Minutes upsets the Highfield Road faithful •1075*

When you speak to Barry Fry, it's like completing a 1,000-piece jigsaw.

Brian Moore on the loquacious doyen of the lower leagues •1076

I have been in some unbelievable scrapes, met some great characters, played at some mad clubs and I wouldn't swap any of it. It's just been a barrel of laughs right from the off.

Steve Claridge on a career in the lower divisions •1077

I'll give you an Arsène Wenger answer – I didn't see the sending-off.
Acting Preston boss Kelham O'Hanlon takes a leaf from the master's book •1078

To be talking about vital games at this stage of the season is ridiculous, really, but tomorrow's game is absolutely vital.
Brian Horton •1079

If we stay there much longer, they might as well rename the league Rochdale Division Three.
Message on the club's official website •1080

People ask "What can John Fashanu bring to Northampton?" In a word, glamour.
John Fashanu's method of becoming Mr Bojangles is to try and buy Northampton Town •1081

I don't want him. I wouldn't mind if we gave him a Mickey Mouse role and he pumped a load of money in.
Bill Beattie, Sheffield Wednesday fan, on the possible appointment of Ken Bates •1082

When you've been thrown out of clubs like Barrow and Southport, you learn to live with disappointment.

Aston Villa's Peter Withe on his omission from Bobby Robson's first England squad •1083

I am manager of Macclesfield and am giving the job my total commitment. Obviously, as an Irishman, I want the job as their international manager.

Sammy McIlroy divides his loyalties •1084

There was Aldershot and training on dog-fouled public parks, where the central midfield player Giorgio Mazzon had a disabled sticker on his car...

Journalist Ian Ridley describes life away from the limelight •1085

It's hard to shake off feeling like a bunch of peasants who found a diamond in the dirt, and then got shoved out the way as a bunch of rich kids pinched it.

Daniel Paul, Plymouth fan, on the loss of manager Paul Sturrock to Southampton. Sturrock, in the end, proved to be mere zirconium •1086

The new stadium helps, and it's something of which I am very proud. It was completed in 1998 to all UEFA and FIFA specifications and seats 3,548 people.

Markus Schaper, general secretary of the Liechtenstein FA •1087

Who's The Bastard In The Black?

All referees are incompetent.
I can't think of a single one
doing a decent job.

The blameless Ian Wright •1088

I never comment on referees
and I'm not going to break the
habit of a lifetime for that prat.

Ron Atkinson with an amusing take on the familiar managerial
bah-humbug response to refereeing decisions •1089

Our passing was poor, we didn't get behind
the ball, but I still blame the referee.

Bryan Robson finds a convenient scapegoat •1090

I shouldn't say what I really feel, but Poll was their best midfielder. You saw him coming off at half-time and he smiled so much he obviously enjoyed that performance.

Sheffield United manager Neil Warnock suggests referee Graham Poll is a gooner, after the Blades' FA Cup semi-final v Arsenal, 2003 •1091

I knew it wasn't going to be our day when I arrived at Links Park and found that we had a woman running the line. She should be at home making the tea or the dinner for her man who comes in after he has been to the football.

Albion Rovers manager Peter Hetherington, on the female official for his side's defeat to Montrose •1092

I know I have been banned for talking about officials, but these days referees have got no bottle – and I thought the linesman was pathetic. *Joe Kinnear* •1093

We had two players sent off at Newcastle last year for heavy breathing. *Joe Royle* •1094

It's a sorry state of affairs when the referee feels he's got equal billing with Eric Cantona. Eric came through his test, I'm not sure the referee did.

Roy Evans on David Elleray after Eric Cantona's first game following a nine-month suspension •1095

I wanted to have a career in sports when I was young, but I had to give it up. I'm only six feet tall, so I couldn't play basketball. I'm only 190 pounds, so I couldn't play football. And I have 20-20 vision, so I couldn't be a referee. *Jay Leno* •1096

I used to talk to the ref but it is easier to see the Pope. If I'm in London next time and I get mugged I hope the same amount of people turn up – there were six police officers, four stewards and a United Nations peace-keeping observer.

Gordon Strachan after a Southampton home defeat •1097

Terrible Senegalese Ref Robs Ghana of a Classic Goal No 3 by Tony Yeboah!

Headline from **Africa Sports** *after a World Cup qualifier in 1992 between Ghana and Algeria* •1098

It's like a toaster, the ref's shirt pocket. Every time there's a tackle, up pops a yellow card.
Kevin Keegan •1099

Referees don't come down here with a particular flavoured shirt on. *Steve Coppell* •1100

Leeds went a goal ahead and, sure enough, the ball boys disappeared.
Ex-referee Keith Hackett notes gamesmanship at Elland Road •1101

A top referee is an official who treats a player like a man. *Ron 'Chopper' Harris* •1102

I do it because I was a useless player.

Jim Rushton on his motivation to make it as a League referee •1103

If you had a linesman on each side of the pitch in both halves you'd have nearly four. *Robbie Earle* •1104

A referee is facing divorce proceedings after he pulled a pair of knickers out of his pocket instead of a red card during a match. Carlos José Figueira Ferro… was so embarrassed that he ended the game with twenty minutes still to go, as his wife, watching, called lawyers…

Report from Terra, Brazil •1105

My dad used to referee me when I was a kid. I remember him booking me – and asking my name. *Coventry's Kevin Kyle* •1106

He can't even control his kids so I wonder
how he can control a game of football.
Referee Howard Webb's wife, Kay, gives his ego a boost
before he takes charge of the 2010 World Cup •1107

Four years' work. A million pounds spent, and what did we get? Two free kicks.

A Brazilian journalist berates the standard of refereeing at
the 1966 World Cup as his country are literally booted out
of the competition •1108

I still don't know if the shot was in or not. I have to say that
I was standing in a poor position for that shot, exactly head-on
instead of diagonal with the goal. I wouldn't have allowed the
goal if Bakhramov hadn't pointed to the middle with his flag.
Gottfried Dienst, 1966 World Cup Final referee, on that goal... •1109

Stalingrad.

Explanation from Azerbaijani linesman
Tofik Bakhramov as to why he gave England's
third, 'on-the-line' goal at the 1966 World Cup Final •1110

You are an Englishman.

German captain Franz Beckenbauer to referee Jack Taylor at the 1974 World Cup Final, after Taylor had awarded Holland a first-minute penalty •1111

The trouble with football referees is that they know the rules but they don't know the game.

Bill Shankly •1112

Shall We Sing A Song For You?

He's fat, he's round, his car is in the pound, Jan Molby.

Variation on a theme after Liverpool's midfielder failed the breathalyser •1113

George, the rabbi wants the ball! Give it 'im!

Wag in the Fulham crowd suggests George Cohen passes to Jimmy Hill •1114

Lenny is a large man sporting a large and frequently unveiled stomach and carrying a briefcase which contains a large pie, presented to raucous cheers from supporters before each game.

Description of unofficial Bradford City mascot Lennie, the City Gent, on fans' website Boys from Brazil •1115

Two pints of Theakstons, a bowl of pie and peas and a cigar… and still change from a fiver!

A seal of approval from a Gillingham fan, drinking in Burnley before a match at Turf Moor •1116

The sky is blue, the clouds are white, God must be a Spireite!
Chesterfield fans claim the Almighty as one of their own •1117

Never felt more like swinging a pig/
from Hyde Park flats, to Wadsley Bridge/
U-ni-ted! You've got me swinging a pig!
Sheffield United fans sing of a local custom •1118

Oh fluffy sheep, are wonderful,
oh fluffy sheep are wonderful.
Because they're white and they're
Welsh, oh fluffy sheep are wonderful.
Wrexham fans bask in the stereotype •1119

Juve! It's just like watching Juve!
*Notts County (Juventus adopted County's black and white stripes when the club
was formed by Englishmen at the beginning of the last century)* •1120

Sing when we're fishing, we
only sing when we're fishing.
Grimsby fans pay tribute to the local industry •1121

269

England have the best fans in the world and Scotland's fans are second to none. *Kevin Keegan* •1122

When they start singing 'You'll Never Walk Alone', my eyes start to water. There have been times when I've actually been crying while I've been playing.
Kevin Keegan on the emotion generated from the Kop •1123

I would rather gouge my eyes out with a rusty spoon than have O'Leary back.
Simon Jose of Leeds United Independent Fans' Association, casts his negative vote •1124

Sort it out Houllier. Not good enough for Liverpool Football Club. No more expensive mistakes. We want the title!
Banner unveiled at Anfield before Liverpool's televised FA Cup tie against Newcastle. They're still waiting... •1125

Manchester United fans can be found in all walks of life. They may smile at you in newsagents' shops or in bus queues. You can find them on parent-teacher associations or in local amateur dramatic societies. They will not be found in the environs of Manchester.
Colin Schindler, writer and Manchester City fan, talking utter tosh •1126

When Rioch came to Millwall we were depressed and miserable. He's done a brilliant job of turning it all around. Now we're miserable and depressed. *Danny Baker on BBC Radio 5 Live's 606* •1127

Although French stadia are more modern, they are used for other things such as athletics. But I prefer British stadia. I prefer the atmosphere here. You are closer to the public. It is warmer, there is room for love.
Eric Cantona on his preference for Portman Road over the Parc des Princes •1128

I just told them — it's not your pitch anyway.
A Gordon Strachan side to Fulham fans after straying from the technical area at Loftus Road •1129

If you can imagine spending five years with an overgrown child clambering about in your attic, then you'll have a fair idea of the impact Graeme Souness has made on Scottish football. **When Saturday Comes** *writer Graham McColl assesses Souness's tenure at Ibrox* •1130

Leicester fan: "It's pantomime season out there!"
Leicester manager Nigel Pearson: "Oh no it isn't!"
Leicester v Southend •1131

We dream of playing in the shirt.
Today God chose you.
Play like the dream.
Banner at the City of Manchester stadium in the days before the Sheikh-up •1132

Beans. Cobi Jones just can't get used to them. Forget the weather, the TV, the accents, the psychopathic full-backs paying him close attention on the mud-laden pitches of the West Midlands. It's the humble products of Heinz, Crosse & Blackwell et al that are causing him real problems. **90 Minutes** *cultural difference facing an American at Coventry* •1133

Can we play you every week?

Portsmouth fans show a sense of humour (and appreciation of the quality of the football on offer) at 5-0 down to Arsenal in an FA Cup quarter-final •1134

Turnip's going up!

*Watford fans' take on Graham Taylor
leading them to promotion* •1135

> You don't understand Newcastle United until you
> understand the hero wears the number 9 shirt.
> *Cardinal Basil Hume is a fan* •1136

I don't understand the rules of football but there are some lovely songs they sing about me.
Mrs Beckham does sarcasm •1137

> I used to stand up and glare around when
> fans were giving Geoff stick and they all used
> to shout, 'Wasn't me Mrs Hurstie, wasn't me'.
> *Geoff Hurst's mother takes on the ICF* •1138

I was in the Leeds end, chanting and going mad, and
the fans were saying 'Hold on, what's he doing here?'
Noel Whelan on playing for and supporting Leeds •1139

If I had to pack the game in tomorrow, I would go
straight out and buy a season ticket for Maine Road…
I grew up in a town that only wanted to know Manchester
United and I've been lucky enough to change that.
City legend Mike Doyle swears his allegiance to the Kippax cause •1140

Joe Jordan strikes quicker than British Leyland.

1970s Scottish banner at Wembley •1141

I looked at the fans and they were singing my name and it made me cry.

Gazza on the moment in Italia '90 when his eyes watered •1142

Cry in a minute, he's going to cry in a minute.

Most opposition crowds to Paul Gascoigne after Italia '90 •1143

There Ain't Nothing Like a James!

Early Highbury chant about Thirties legend Alex James, based on the popular song, "There Ain't Nothin' Like a Dame!" •1144

We're supposed to be at home.

Brighton fans at the Priestfield Stadium after being forced to play their home games at Gillingham •1145

116 years of tradition ended.

Message on wreath delivered by those unwilling to accept Rangers' signing of the Catholic Maurice Johnston •1146

All I Want for Christmas is a Dukla Prague Away Kit
Title of 1986 single from Half Man Half Biscuit •1147

We've lost that Terry Phelan, ohhh-woh Terry Phelan. We've lost that Terry Phelan, now it's Vonk, Vonk, Vonk.

Manchester City fans take a huge liberty with the Righteous Brothers You've Lost That Loving Feeling *as Terry Phelan is replaced by Michael Vonk* •1148

Man offers marriage proposal to any woman with ticket for Leeds United v Sheffield United game. Must send photograph (of ticket).

Advert placed in the Yorkshire Evening Post *before a vital Second Division clash in 1990* •1149

Communism v Alcoholism

Caledonian banner at the USSR v Scotland game in the 1982 World Cup finals •1150

Phil Neville should have his passport confiscated and not be allowed to leave the country.
England fan Scott Vessey gets things a little out of proportion after Neville's concession of a late penalty knocks England out of Euro 2000 •1151

We hate you so much because we loved you so much.

Barcelona banner on Luís Figo's first game at the Nou Camp after transferring to Real Madrid •1152

Never again fascism! Never again war! Never again Third Division!
The fans from Hamburg outfit St. Pauli get their priorities right •1153

Liverpool – 30 miles from greatness

Visiting Man United fans unveil a banner at Anfield •1154

Bjørn-e-bye in my gang, my gang, my gang

Reprise of the Gary Glitter tune by Blackburn fans to Stig Inge Bjørnebye •1155

Donkey won the derby!

Arsenal fans' chant after Tony Adams scored the winner against Spurs •1156

I was given shirt number 50 at the start of
the season. They thought it was a safe one
to allocate but new signing Nikos Dabizas
has taken Micky Adams' squad to 44.
So, if he makes five more signings, I'll be
in the reckoning and could get a game.

Leicester City mascot Filbert Fox gets his hopes up •1157

Live round the corner, you only live round the corner.

Universal chant to Manchester United away fans •1158

He's fat, he's round, he's never in the ground, Captain Bob.

Oxford (and Derby) fans' question the attendance record of chairman Robert Maxwell •1159

Come in a taxi, you must have come in a taxi.
Sung to any small groups of away fans. **Various** •1160

> Park, Park, wherever you may be /
> You eat dogs in your home country /
> Could be worse, could be a scouse /
> Eating rats in your council house.
> *Manchester United fans ditty to Ji Sung Park* •1161

One Mrs Zola, there's only one Mrs Zola.

Chelsea fans thank Gianfranco's spouse after she reportedly persuaded hubby to stay at Stamford Bridge for another season •1162

Give us back our bicycles.

Dutch chant against Germany during Euro '88, a reference to the Nazis' mass confiscation of the nation's bikes during World War II •1163

279

You can't see your willy, you can't see your willy, la la la la.
A Stamford Bridge chorus to a rotund Oxford goalkeeper •1164

Woolwich rejects.
Charlton taunt to former South Londoners Arsenal •1165

Flats on the Cottage, they're building flats on the Cottage.
Aimed at Fulham fans since their departure to Loftus Road •1166

Tell me ma, me ma, To put the champagne on ice, We're going to Wembley twice.
Everton fans murder Doris Day during a particularly good cup season •1167

We are Millwall, we are Millwall, no-one likes us, we don't care.
Lions' fans adopt a spot of self-analysis •1168

Georgie Best, superstar. Walks like a woman and he wears a bra.

Early example of derogatory chant •1169

Kick it off, throw it in, have a little scrimmage, Keep it low, splendid rush, bravo, win or die.

Start of curious and quaint chant still sung at Carrow Road •1170

David James, superstar, drops more bollocks than Grobelaar. *Manchester United fans at Anfield* •1171

Have you got another kit?

Southampton fans bait Manchester United, one season after Fergie had blamed their defeat on the apparent camouflageable quality of a new grey strip •1172

We'll really shake 'em up/ when we win the World Cup/ 'cos Scotland is the greatest football team.

From Ally's Tartan Army by Andy Cameron, 1978. We all know what happened next •1173

If you've all got a passport clap your hands.

Sung to Mohammad Al Fayed while waving British passport above head •1174

The first time I got the ball for a throw-in the fans were all shouting at me "What have you done to your hair?"
Chris Waddle on the first appearance of his infamous mullet •1175

One team in Tallinn. There's only one team in Tallinn.

Scottish fans at the World Cup qualifier in Estonia. After a protest over the kick-off time, Scotland kicked off against no opposition •1176